Adirondack
Cabin Country

York State
BOOKS

Paul Schaefer

Ever since I was a young man, Adirondack wilderness has called me. Even then, I knew that I would devote my life to keeping these mountains wild and free. Photograph by Leo Franklin.

Adirondack Cabin Country

Paul Schaefer

Edited by
Noel Riedinger-Johnson

Syracuse University Press

Copyright © 1993 by Paul Schaefer
All Rights Reserved

First Edition 1993
93 94 95 96 97 98 99   6 5 4 3 2 1

The paper used in this publication meets the minimum requirements of
American National Standard for Information Sciences . . . Permanence of
paper for Printed Library Materials, ANSI Z39.48-1984. ∞™

Library of Congress Cataloging-in-Publication Data
Schaefer, Paul.
  Adirondack cabin country / Paul Schaefer ; edited by Noel
Riedinger-Johnson
     p.   cm.—(York State books)
  ISBN 0-8156-0275-8 (pbk.)
     1. Natural history—New York (State)—Adirondack Park. 2. Natural
history—New York (State)—Adirondack Forest Preserve. 3. Natural
history—New York (State)—Adirondack Mountain Reserve. 4. Nature
conservation—New York (State)—Adirondack Park. 5. Nature
conservation—New York (State)—Adirondack Forest Preserve.
6. Nature conservation—New York (State)—Adirondack Mountain
Reserve. I. Riedinger-Johnson, Noel. II. Title.
QH105.N7S35 1993
508.747'5—dc20   93-8538

Manufactured in the United States of America

Dedicated to the memories of

Peter A. Schaefer

my father, who climbed the Alps in Austria and Switzerland, and who led us and encouraged our activities in the great outdoors, and to

Rose A. Schaefer

my mother, who reached similar heights in spirit, who made possible our lifelong adventures, and who encouraged all of our efforts in the conservation of natural resources.

Paul Schaefer has been a visionary leader of the New York State conservation movement since his early twenties. During his long career, he has served on countless advisory committees for state and private agencies. His numerous awards and honors include the Governor Nelson A. Rockefeller Award from the New York State Conservation Council (1966), the Conservationist of the Year Award from International Safari (1969), the Chevron USA Award (1985), the Conservationist of the Year Award from the Adirondack Council (1985), the Governor Mario Cuomo Conservation Award (1985), and the Alexander Calder Conservation Award (1990). He was involved with the passage of the National Wilderness Act of 1964 and for eleven years edited *The Forest Preserve* magazine. In 1979, Union College recognized his outstanding contributions to conservation by awarding him an honorary doctor of science degree. His most recent book, *Defending the Wilderness: The Adirondack Writings of Paul Schaefer* (Syracuse University Press, 1989), documents the campaign of more than half a century to preserve the wilderness in the Adirondacks.

With a cherished whiskered mountain man I have kindled a tiny campfire under the evergreens on the shore of a lake most folks seem to have forgotten. The dry spruce limbs blaze quickly and send sparks into the dark night air. Miles and miles of forest are between us and a highway, and trees climb in unbroken ranks from the shoreline up the mountains. There is an almost imperceptible sound of waves lapping on the shore. A light breeze whispers through branches overhead. From the far end of the lake, a loon shatters the quiet with its yodel-like cry. Another one answers, as it flies in front of us, heading toward that end of the lake.

There is a stillness that hangs over the land. We are reluctant to break it. The fire continues to send sparks into the night and casts flickering shadows on the surrounding trees. There is a melody in the silence. An owl breaks the stillness. The mountain man looks at me with a smile and raises his hand. Then all is quiet again.

Contents

x / Contents

Illustrations

Foreword

Norman J. Van Valkenburgh

Who has not, in a moment of frustration, in the midst of a
family squabble, or when all seemed to be going wrong,
wanted to get away from it all? Who has not, when over-
whelmed by the din of traffic from the streets outside, the
incessant jangle of the telephone, or the mindless blare from
some nearby television set, wished to be a part of the quiet and
solitude of some remote spot out in the Back-of-Beyond? Who
has not, at least once, wanted to give it all up and head for a
cabin in the woods?

Some did, of course. Thoreau built a cabin on the shore
of Walden Pond. But that was nearly in his own backyard, so
he really didn't get away from much of anything. John Burroughs
tried a number of retreats. At "Riverby," his home on the west
shore of the Hudson River at West Park, he used what he
called his "back-covered study," in reality a cabin hidden in the
trees on a knoll away from the house. Later on, he built
"Slabsides" in the hills behind West Park, and it was in this
rustic cabin that he most enjoyed receiving his visitors. At the
family homestead, which he named "Woodchuck Lodge," near
Roxbury in the Catskills, Burroughs moved out of the house
and did his writing in the "hay-barn study" to get away from
the women, who, he thought, talked too much.

But it is the Adirondack cabin that stirs the imagination. Certainly, these mountains have known their share of hermits, rusticators, and traditionalists who sought to withdraw from society for a time. But they have also known writers, who looked for seclusion for one reason or another and found that the attraction of these rugged hills, the closeness of nature, and the tranquility of a cabin around them evoked thoughts and words that came easily to the written page.

Robert Louis Stevenson came to the Adirondacks in the winter of 1887-1888 seeking a quiet place where he could find relief for his sufferings from pulmonary tuberculosis. He chose the sanitarium colony at Saranac Lake. His "cabin" was a small rented house on the fringe of the then somewhat primitive hamlet. Nevertheless, it was "on a hill," said Stevenson in a letter to a friend, "and has sight of a stream turning a corner in the valley . . . and sees some hills too." Here Stevenson wrote twelve essays, some other short pieces, and most of the first draft of *The Master of Ballantrae.*

Edward Zane Carroll Judson's tales were on a less-lofty plane, but he was a writer all the same. He came to the Adirondacks in 1859 and built a cabin on the north shore of Eagle Lake, westerly from Blue Mountain Lake. His fame came from his writings under the penname of Ned Buntline and his glamorization of Buffalo Bill. He called his cabin "Eagle's Nest," and there he turned out penny dreadfuls and one poem about the Adirondacks that was nothing less than an adoration of his "wildwood home."

Verplanck Colvin sometimes wrote his journals in a tent out on the transit line as he led his intrepid band of surveyors along the intricacies of the patents and grants that divided these northern hills. It was on one Adirondack summit in 1870 that he had his vision of a grand "Adirondack Park or timber preserve." It was his persistence, written in the pages of his annual reports, that finally persuaded the New York State Legislature to create the Adirondack Park. Colvin's tent may not have been as permanent as a cabin, but his own sturdiness made up for that. Regardless, it was the country outside his tent that captured his soul.

The greatest writings ever to be inspired by the Adirondack Mountains may have been Howard Zahniser's sixty-six drafts of the federal wilderness bill. The last draft was signed into law by President Lyndon Johnson on September 3, 1964, as the National Wilderness Preservation Act, just four months after Zahniser's death. Although he did not write every word of every draft in his cabin on the fringe of what is now the Siamese Ponds Wilderness Area, it was the surrounding mountains and this part of the Adirondack Forest Preserve that inspired him. It is no small coincidence that Zahniser's neighbor, just over the hill, and his companion on those hikes into the High Peaks was Paul Schaefer.

Just what is this curious piece of the world that is the Adirondack Park and the Adirondack Forest Preserve, two terms used interchangeably by many who don't understand what either is all about? The distinction is simple: The forest preserve is the state-owned land and water (with some exceptions) in the twelve Adirondack counties; the park is all the land and water inside a blue line drawn on a map to enclose something less than the twelve counties. The New York State Forest Preserve came into being under an 1885 law and now amounts to nearly 3 million acres. The Adirondack Park was created by law in 1892 and now amounts to nearly 6 million acres, almost 50 percent of which is state-owned or forest preserve and the rest of which is privately owned.

It is this intermixing of state and private land ownerships that makes the Adirondacks unique. It is why campaigners are needed to wage the battles necessary to maintain the balance and assure that the state lands remain as nature intended. It is why writers are needed to tell of the wonders of these forested hills and the entrancement of them. Paul Schaefer is both, and the rest of us are the beneficiaries of his willingness to sacrifice, from time to time, his family and his chance for fortune in his lifelong fight on the side of the Adirondack wilderness.

Paul Schaefer is no stranger to Adirondackers near and far. He is the defender of what they hold dear. Although he himself rejects the image, others see him as a knight errant astride a white horse, Adirondack guidon flying, routing those who would profane that country loved by them and by him. He once told me he wouldn't spend an overnight outside New York State because someone, hearing he was gone, might do something untoward to the Adirondacks before he could return in the morning. A defender? Indeed!

In fact, his recent book is entitled *Defending the Wilderness* (Syracuse University Press, 1989). It is an anthology of some of his writings describing his jousts with bureaucrats, frauds, deceivers, and bamboozlers who propounded ideas and plans they said would "improve" the Adirondacks. Ironically, one of the most pitched of these battles was over the so-called closed–cabin scheme. This ill-conceived plan proposed an amendment to (then) ARTICLE VII of the New York State Constitution, which declared the New York State Forest Preserve was to be "forever kept as wild forest lands," to allow New York State to construct paths, trails, campsites, and camping facilities on those hollowed grounds in the Adirondacks and Catskills and the "making of necessary clearings therefore."

The whole thing seemed rather innocuous—after all, much of what was proposed was being done already—and the amendment breezed through the 1930 and 1931 legislatures. However, some sharp-eyed guardians of the forest preserve, Paul Schaefer and his mentor, John S. Apperson, read the amendment more closely than others and found a loophole that would permit the building of cabin colonies, dance halls, hot-dog stands, and even worse anywhere in the forest preserve. They mobilized the believers, spread the truth, and the amendment went down to defeat at the polls in November of 1932 by a two-to-one margin.

Like that defense of the wilderness, the other campaigns he waged left no doubt about Paul Schaefer's goals. He was a protector of the forest preserve and the Adirondack Park, and he was in it for the long haul. That his zeal and lifelong love affair with the Adirondacks have not waned is the mark of the dedication he has brought to his cause.

The Adirondacks are a big place and seem too large for one person to grasp, however. Is it possible that Paul has some special part of the realm that is his true love? Is it possible that Paul has his own secret place and his own cabin there where he rests from his battles and writes about them in an attempt to compel the rest of us to join with him? He told us this might be so in *Defending the Wilderness*.

He begins the second essay in the first part of that book by telling of his first visit to the Adirondacks at the age of twelve. In order to help restore the health of his mother, the family went to stay "at the home of a mountain guide" on the edge of what is now the Siamese Ponds Wilderness, and the die was cast. He "thrived in this wild country" and a few years later he and his brother Vince "bought an ancient log cabin and seven acres of land with a mountain stream." He then says, with deep feeling, "the lure of this cabin country was irresistible." A good thing for all of us that it was.

Cabin Country is different from *Defending the Wilderness*. Paul used his earlier book to tell how he fought the good fight. This one tells why. The earlier book sets the stage. This one takes Paul to his rightful place alongside Burroughs and Thoreau as a chronicler of the enchantment of the natural world and of the reasons it should be preserved.

Paul now tells us about his special place and the people there who shared his growing up and educated him in its ways and mysteries, and we are the better for it. Come along on this narrative journey to Cabin Country. You will find it not to be some mythical place nor made up of cabins in the sky. You will be glad Paul Schaefer is your guide through the pages, and you will soon realize that your travels are not from, but to reality.

Acknowledgments

Throughout the years many, many people have helped me complete my conservation work and the various projects associated with it. *Adirondack Cabin Country* is no exception. Noel Riedinger-Johnson has helped me in one way or another for more than twenty years. She wrote and edited our documentary film, *The Adirondack: The Land Nobody Knows*. After she edited Jeanne Robert Foster's *Adirondack Portraits: A Piece of Time*, she encouraged me to put together *Defending the Wilderness* and edited the manuscript. This time, I handed her pages of writing and photographs, and she returned to me a completed manuscript that turned my work into a book. To her I am indebted.

Colleen Bodane typed my hand written pages into her computer, returned typed pages for review and revision, and forwarded computer disks to Noel.

Nancy Kates transferred Colleen's disks to an IBM-compatible computer, retyped my typewritten material into the computer, and prepared disks for Noel. She also trimmed photographs and proofread the final manuscript.

I also want to thank the many individuals who have permitted me over the years to use their photographs to supplement my own extensive collection and to include their work (credited throughout the book) in this publication.

Paul Schaefer

Historical Perspective

Engineers and surveyors of the British War Office in London in 1775 produced a map entitled "British Northern Colonies" for use by their military forces invading North America. The map included about 15,000 square miles of northern New York State, which they designated "Couchsachrage." The rivers and lakes that bounded this great wilderness tract were clearly delineated, for they were the only highways available for the military of either England or France to use in their quest to possess an empire in North America. Left blank on the map were the 7 million acres enclosed by the St. Lawrence River on the north and northwest, Lake Champlain on the east, the Mohawk River on the south, and Lake Ontario on the west. A subsequent map stated "this vast tract of land . . . has not yet been surveyed."

Control of these near-sea-level boundary waters was pivotal to the military success of the countries involved. In 1609, Samuel de Champlain discovered the lake that bears his name and began a conflict that was not settled for one and one-half centuries. During those first days of discovery, he and his Algonquin Indians fought a successful battle against an Iroquois war party near the south end of the lake. From that day on, the powerful Iroquois nation fought the French and eventually became allies of the English.

Major battles were fought on and along these strategic rivers and lakes. A single battle in 1758 cost the English and

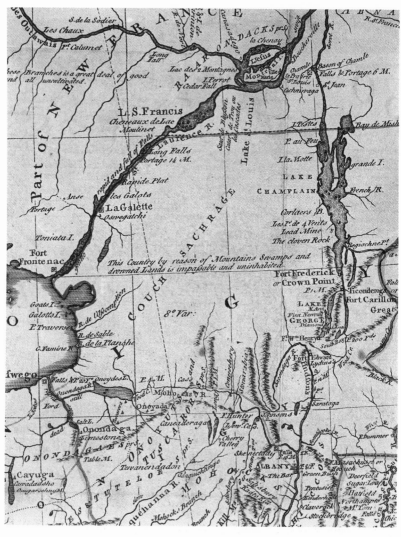

1775 British War Map

Printed map of Couchsachrage, or "Beaver Hunting Country of the Iroquois," prepared by the British Engineers and Surveyors of the War Office in 1775. The region was named the "Adirondack Group" by Ebenezer Emmons, the New York State geologist, in 1837.

their allies more than 2,000 dead out of an army of 15,000 during one day of fighting the French at Fort Ticonderoga.

As a result of decades of bloody fighting between the English, French, and the original Dutch settlers, possession of the North American continent began to crystallize by 1770. The English defeated the French at Quebec, and Canada became a part of England's global empire. When the American Revolution stripped England of the thirteen colonies and ended its military influence on the continent, New York State acquired the seven million acres of land north of the Mohawk River. This was the Couchsachrage region outlined on the invasion map of 1775.

When peace came to an exhausted state, exploration of the unmapped wilderness region began. Hunters and trappers began moving up the scores of rivers and streams that cut into the wilderness. They found that the rivers rose in the center of the region and radiated like wheel spokes to the boundary waters.

From Maine to Georgia the only level water route to the west was the Mohawk River. De Witt Clinton, the visionary governor of New York, decided in 1813 to build a canal more than 350 miles in length west from Albany to the Great Lakes. The canal was completed in 1825, and immigrants in packets pulled by horses or mules had a way to reach the fertile lands of the great American west. They bypassed the wilderness north of the Mohawk. In a similar fashion, the immigrants who sailed up the St. Lawrence River also bypassed this same wilderness.

The land north of the Mohawk remained a mystery for generations. In a special article on the topography of New York published in the 1830 report of the Albany Institute, a noted geologist had this to say:

> The second division of the mountain district of the state, or that on the north side of the Mohawk and Oneida valley, and Lake Champlain, has not been as minutely explored by topographic surveys . . . as the district we have

already described. One of the peaks . . . called the White
Face, rises to a height of 1686 feet.

The mountains of this section are often described as
an isolated group, entirely disconnected by the Appala-
chian system, which is generally considered as terminating
in New York, at the valley of the Mohawk River and
Oneida Lake. But when we view their relative positions,
and the general direction of their several ridges, we must
at once be convinced that they are, with all other mountains of the state, only part of the great chain which
traverses the United States from Alabama to Maine. Indeed, the existence of a separate mountain group in any
part of our national territory, has been reasonably doubted,
and strictly speaking such a phenomenon is perhaps not
to be found on the surface of the globe.

The conclusions reached by this geologist on these lands
could scarely be more incorrect. For the mountains of
Couchsachrage were not of the Applachian system. They are a
unique and isolated part of the Canadian Shield. The height of
Whiteface is 3,000 feet higher than he claimed it to be. And the
sketch of the topography of the state illustrating his article
inaccurately shows the Catskills as being twice as high as these
mountains. This is a classic example of the lack of knowledge
of northern New York at that time.

Seven years after the Albany Institute report, Ebenezer
Emmons, New York State geologist, discovered the highest peak
in the mountains to be more than a mile above sea level and
named it Mount Marcy after the governor who authorized his
survey. He also gave the term "Adirondack Group" to the
hundreds of mountains that stretched in all directions from
that peak to far horizons.

In 1868, a young man from Albany named Verplanck
Colvin began the exploration (an odyssey that spanned more
than thirty years) and mapping of this great region. His discoveries and reports to the legislature in a series of dramatic books
became a basis for the establishment of the New York State

The ADIRONDACKS ... CARVED BY THE GLACIERS OR THE ICEBERGS OF THE DRIFT PERIOD FROM THE MOST ANCIENT GRANITE OF THE WORLDS FORMATION: WASHED AND ERODED BY THE STORMS OF A THOUSAND CENTURIES, THE ADIRONDACK RANGES RISE IN DARK AND GLOOMY BILLOWS, STRETCHING FROM THE HILLS WHICH SKIRT THE MOHAWK AWAY NORTHWARD TO THE SHORES OF THAT RIVER FROM WHICH THIS MOST ANCIENT ROCK TAKES THE TERM LAURENTIAN. ELSEWHERE ARE MOUNTAINS MORE STUPENDOUS, MORE ICY AND MORE DREAR ; BUT NONE LOOK DOWN UPON A GRANDER LANDSCAPE, IN RICH AUTUMN TIME : MORE BRIGHTLY GEMMED OR JEWELED WITH INNUMERABLE LAKES, OR CRYSTAL POOLS, OR WILD WITH SAVAGE CHASMS OR DREAD PASSES ; NONE SHOW A DENSER OR MORE VAST APPEARANCE OF PRIMEVAL FOREST STRETCHED OVER RANGE UPON RANGE TO THE FAR HORIZON, WHERE THE SEA OF PEAKS FADE INTO A DIM, VAPOROUS UNCERTAINTY. A REGION OF MYSTERY, OVER WHICH NONE CAN GAZE WITHOUT A STRANGE THRILL OF INTEREST AND OF WONDER AT WHAT MIGHT BE HIDDEN IN THAT VAST AREA OF FOREST, COVERING ALL THINGS WITH ITS DEEP REPOSE.

Verplanck Colvin. 1879

Adirondack Relief Map

This relief map of the Adirondack Park covers most of the land designated Couchsachrage *by the British War Office in 1775 and was completed about two hundred years after the original map was printed by the British military. The map required nine years of volunteer work by fifty individuals under the direction of the Friends of the Forest Preserve. They used the technology of the U.S. Corps of Engineers, who built maps for the invasion forces in the South Pacific during World War II. Photograph by Thomas Carney.*

Forest Preserve in 1885, the creation of the Adirondack Park in 1892, and the now-famous "forever wild" covenant in the New York State Constitution that prohibits lumbering in the forest preserve. His accomplishments are an important part of the foundation of the Adirondack Park as it exists today.

Before Colvin's day, an impoverished New York had been disposing of the 7 million acres of wilderness it owned to lumber barons. As a result, some of the great forests protecting the sources of the state's major rivers and streams were devastated by logging and subsequent forest fires. By the time Colvin began his work for the state in 1872, fewer than 40,000 acres remained in state ownership. Dry stream beds and ravaging floods gave emphasis to his clarion calls for the protection of the vital watershed forests.

Coincidentally with the publication of Colvin's reports to the legislature, there came an avalanche of books, maps, articles, and photographs of the region by historians, sportsmen, and journalists. These materials encouraged voluminous reports by state agencies between 1885 and 1910 that contain a treasure of information.

As strange as it seems, despite all that had been written and published for generations, in 1921 Alfred L. Donaldson began his otherwise magnificent work, *A History of the Adirondacks,* with "The Adirondacks are a group of mountains in northeastern New York. . . . There are about one hundred peaks ranging from 1,200 feet to 5,000 feet in height." In actuality, the Adirondacks contain more than 2,000 mountains, 2,700 lakes, and 30,000 miles of rivers and streams.

Misinformation about New York's vast northern wilderness that was published well into the twentieth century is indicative of the lack of knowledge about the region that existed at that time. It was during the 1920s that I came to the Adirondacks and began my lifelong adventure with the mountains—their forests, lakes, rivers, and wetlands. I came with the spirit of adventure that drives youth. Fortunately, visionary leaders of the state had set aside these wild forest lands, and there was still a frontier to explore at a time when much of the other wild lands in the United States had already given way to destruction and development. My early journeys into the wild with mountain people who lived with the land awakened a reverence for this unknown region. Since those early years, I have spent my life learning about the Adirondacks and fighting to keep the mountains and rivers in their natural state so that there will always be a frontier for youth to explore.

North to the Adirondacks

Crane Mountain

Crane Mountain dominates Cabin Country. From its isolated summit in the east-central Adirondacks that rises more than 3,000 feet above the sea-level waters of Lake Champlain, you can see the High Peaks of the Adirondacks to the north; the Champlain Valley and Vermont's Green Mountains to the northeast; Garnet Lake and the Silver Lake Wilderness to the south; and Cataract and Gore mountains and the Siamese Ponds Wilderness to the west. On a very clear day, you can see the Catskill Mountains.

On the western shoulder of the mountains, cliffs flank the shore of a glacial trout lake, and the outlet of the lake drops nearly 1,000 feet into the isolated and historic Elliot Putnam farm.

The land I call "cabin country" is a tiny east central part of the historic Adirondack mountain region. It is a microcosm of innumerable similar regions in the Adirondacks that have places scarcely known even today. There are mountaintops jeweled with tiny lakes; there are cataracts seldom seen; there are trackless swamps and regions without trails except those made by denizens of the forest. It is a land untrammeled by man where nature remains untamed.

The pioneers who first settled these upland acres above the hamlet of Baker's Mills left scant records of their lives except for the clearings and far views of distant mountains. They led a life that was harsh and frugal. An old log cabin still stands along the trail into the wilderness. And here and there beyond the present clearings on the edge of the wilderness are evidences of barns that once dominated the fields that the forest has now reclaimed.

Thin soils and short growing seasons discouraged farming. To augment scanty crops, the settlers worked long months in logging camps deep in the woods and risked their lives riding logs on roaring rivers that brought them to the mills. They also ran long traplines for beaver and other furbearers and became guides for hunters and fishermen who began to reach these remote parts of the state. Their hardscrabble life, shared by women and children, had compensations in the freedom they knew. Some of their graves are on almost forgotten hillsides that reveal only a depression in the earth and have no marker to identify their occupants.

Into this country in 1921 came our family of seven—straight from the streets of a Schenectady in the Capital District. There was Father, who had climbed the Alps, and Mother, who despite her precarious health was always the life of the family. I was a youngster of thirteen, with two brothers and two sisters.

Transportation to this remote region, then accessible only by dirt roads, was by means of two rather ancient vehicles. One, a roadster, was driven by one of my father's friends. The other car was a Model T Ford driven by an uncle who had hunted this region. He had arranged for us to occupy for the summer the wing of a house that belonged to a guide he knew. The house was at an elevation of 2,000 feet, close to a towering mountain and the edge of wilderness. My uncle believed that this high mountain country with its invigorating atmosphere would be beneficial to Mother's health.

All of us found that the lives we had been living were dramatically changed. The people living in the few houses at the edge of the wilderness were refreshingly different from those we knew in the city. Two miles down the road, Baker's Mills had a general store, church, the remains of a mill, and a few houses. The hamlet was on the historic dirt road from North Creek to Wells, twenty-miles distant through the woods and along a river.

Our nearest neighbor was Johnny Morehouse. He shared his scanty fare with our family. Milk, eggs, rutabagas (called " 'beggies"), maple syrup, and berries were lifesavers for us. We had trout once in a while, an occasional woodchuck, and sometimes deer and bear.

My first summer there was a dream. The surrounding forest was so vast, so ominous as to make me fear it, and at the same time, eager to explore it. My first impressions of the country were mostly ones of awe. Tales of the great forest that lay unbroken westerly for miles, of men who got lost there, and the fact that it was inhabited by deer and bear—all these intrigued me. The natives were a breed I had never met before. They were hunters, trappers, fishermen, loggers, and guides. They led what seemed to me to be a carefree life despite an almost total lack of money and undeniable hardscrabble conditions. I especially enjoyed the nights they fiddled and had square dances in the house we lived in.

I was seldom idle. I helped cut wood, drove cows to pasture, and was involved in all the other things that were part of a frugal mountain life. The natives responded to my interest in their activities, and soon they would take me into the bordering wilderness, to lakes and streams and beaver ponds. At the end of the first ten weeks, a genuine appreciation of their life was so embedded in me that I hated to go home to school.

Thereafter, I was the envy of my chums to whom I related my mountain adventures. Each year as soon as school was out, we headed north. After two years, my father was able to buy a small house a short distance from our mountaineer's home. This made the adventures more complete. Getting older, I gradually gained confidence in myself because of my trips with the natives back in the wilderness. When necessity forced me to quit school and work as an apprentice carpenter, my weekend trips to Cabin Country became more frequent. Ever since then, the lure of this mountain country has been irresistible!

Throughout the years, I have always tried to capture my wilderness adventures in writing and started with a series of essays in the 1920s. These early essays, written between 1921 and 1932, reflect my growing awareness of the mountain culture and the people there who helped to mold my love for the mountains. The stories here are a sampling of the great adventures I have had with just a few of the people who made this region all that it means to me.

Garnet Lake

Garnet Lake from the top of Crane Mountain, with the Silver Lake Wilderness in the distance. Photograph by Dan Ling.

The Ancient Call

As far back as I can remember, I have been prey to that old, old passion—the love for adventure. I think one of my ancestors must have been a sturdy pioneer who knew the lure of the golden west and the great Uncertain beyond the setting sun. My love to breast a fresh mountain breeze and to look at the bluish hills or far horizons have been a part of me since childhood.

About one-half mile from my boyhood home was a dense woods nearly one-half-mile square, the former estate of a wealthy family. The mansion was situated deep in the woods near a spot overlooking the beautiful Mohawk Valley and the river that threads its way through fertile lowlands. When I was about ten, the owners died, and the place was left to disintegrate. In due time, the ghosts of the owners came back, or so we were told, and the place became haunted.

Relatives of the original owners posted the estate, and everyone was strictly forbidden to set foot on the grounds. For that very reason, my friends and I decided the place was fully worthy of our explorations. We discovered huge chestnut trees, fine coasting and skiing hills, and signs that skunks and rabbits infested the place. It was an ideal site for our rendezvous.

In a short time, by virtue of much hard work before and after school, we had a crude hut built and a name for every hill and gully. We were enjoying all the thrills of pioneer life. Also over the hill and down in a deep gully next to a railroad track,

7

there was a crystal cold spring and a gathering place for vagabonds who rode the rails. This added an exciting dimension to the whole place. We blazed trails through the woods, one of which gave us sight of the vagabonds' campfire, where we often saw a large pot of stew steaming from forked sticks above it.

From our rendezvous, we could look far across the valley to the blue hills north of the river, the foothills of the Adirondacks. Occasionally, we would see a hunter returning from those hills, and we always gaped wonderingly at the stories he told. I will never forget the night one nimrod was discovered coming up our trail with a fox over his shoulder. Upon seeing how much he claimed of our adimiration, he began telling us tales of the Adirondacks, where he had hunted deer, bear, and wildcat. Needless to day, we had many wild dreams after he left our campfire that night. I doubt that the hunter ever fully realized how famous he had become.

As we grew older, we entered the Lone Scouts of America and began to look for new fields to conquer. Gradually, our hikes, encouraged by my father, grew longer. The Sand Plains, Tippecanoe, and the hills we had looked toward over our schoolbooks began yielding new and more interesting discoveries. The Plotterkill, which in springtime roars down a heavily wooded valley four miles below Twin Upland Falls to the Mohawk River, took up most of our time. Camping trips became the rule, and overnight excursions were a never-ending source of pleasure.

Gaining confidence in myself in the woods and afield, occasionally I would take a "hermit hike" as my parents called it. I enjoyed these trips immensely. They permitted me to range and roam at will, to sit on a hilltip and dream when I cared to, and to uncover many facts of nature heretofore unknown to me.

One fine autmn day when I was about twelve my meanderings brought me to a gove of tall red pines, high in the Plotterkill hills. Several hundred feet below, the stream was in white water, while to the north the foothills of the Adirondacks were seen. The uncommonness of the red pines held me fascinated for a time; and although still awed by the beauty of the spot, I caught a glimpse of a log cabin nestling in the evergreens.

The elation of the discovery remains vivid. After a hasty inspection convinced me it had long since been abandoned, I turned toward home to report my wonder find to my chums. I ran most of the way. I forgot to tell them that the roof was full of holes, that the walls were sagging, and that the stove had probably seen its best days. We immediately agreed that I was to lead an expedition there at the earliest opportunity.

The following Saturday we were there. It was raining. Depsite the deterioration and a stove that almost smoked us out, we decided to fix the cabin up. In the process, a dream developed—one day I would have a cabin in the Adirondacks, far beyond those hills beckoning to the north.

It would be situated on some mountain's height, where I could look off to a peak-studded horizon. A tumbling brook would be nearby. The wilderness would reach out to embrace it. A lovely peak would stand in silent guard above it. Lakes and rivers and streams would be near. Deer antlers would hang over the door, and a bear rug would grace the floor.

Guns, traps, and other treasures of the long trails
would litter the cabin.

Hugh Lackey

The Mountaineers

Hi thar! Wanta go up yonder mountain with me after a sheep?" Tall, lanky, kindly old Hugh leaned on his long barreled rifle one lazy, hazy September morn and grinned at me as I was splitting some kindling.

Junipers! Would I go! As if any red-blooded fifteen-year-old boy could resist such a chance for adventure! The great hulking mountains that surrounded our camp always beckoned; however, up to this point I had been unable to overcome the vague fear of them I seemed to have. A great part of this fear was perhaps caused by, what seemed to me now, the sheltered life that I had led in the city. Certainly, life in the backwoods settlement that mother had come to for her health was entirely new and different to us all. It almost seemed as if I were living on a different planet altogether when I thought of the hustling, bustling, noisy place that I had left so recently. Something in the very air seemed to intensify a spirit of languidness that so many of the natives seemed to be endowed with. Consequently, it was no hardship for me to forget the kindling and the work that it involved for the time being. I was well acquainted with Hugh Lackey, the old mountaineer, because of the appeal that his jig-fiddling held for me; however, this was the first time that he had ever invited me to go along on a mountain trip with him.

Like every mountaineer that I have met, Hugh is a singular character. Men are all individuals in the Adirondacks, and

11

each one appears to be so different from the other. Typifying that easy-going, carefree existence of the hills that so many Adirondackers seem to possess, Hugh is also blessed with a deep sense of dry humor. He is powerfully built; and even though his shoulders appear to be a bit narrow, I would not underestimate his strength. Hugh stands six-feet-two in his socks, and he has a cunning little way of always forgetting "perzakly" just how old he is. The wrinkles in his face seem to add to his character; and because he spends so much of his life in the great outdoors, he does not lose his suntan from one season to the next. His skin resembles bronzed leather. I have seldom seen him wearing a shirt with sleeves that did not end several inches above his wrists, and I have never seen him when his trousers were not rolled a third of the way to his knees.

Hugh knew that he did not have to wait for me to accept his invitation to go up the mountain with him; and he was so sure what my reaction would be that he added, "Tell yer Maw we'll git back whin we git some meat. Mebby before!" We were soon headed for some barren, rocky fields on the lower rugged slopes of Height-of-Land Mountain. Our objective was to bring down one of a band of domesticated mountain sheep that had felt the urge of their ancestors and had returned to native haunts, which were rugged but lacked the precipitous crags of their true homeland. It was considered good stalking to get one of this dwindling band, for their domestication had not impaired their keen senses of sight and smell.

Hugh is a woodsman par excellence and is considered as good a shot as the hills can produce. His long, easy stride was a thing of awe to me at this time. I marveled at his ability to traverse the woods so noiselessly. After crossing several fields, waist high with brambles, we came upon an old sugar-camp trail. The trail was flanked on both sides with a luxuriant growth of ferns. A few red maples were daubed with scarlet and gold, for autumn was fast stripping summer of her laurels. We slowly worked our way up the trail, and it seemed that we climbed into the sky. There were no fences, and civilization seemed to be a thing of dim, remote reminiscence. Something deep within me responded to the whole thing. Panting, I distinctly remember the exhilaration and the exultation when I realized that a lifelong hunger was being satisfied!

At length, we emerged into one of the barren, rocky fields that we had seen from the valley. Hugh began to examine the ground and shortly came to this conclusion, "Musta jist sceered the critters. They bedded down over thar last noight. See this." His hand waved in the direction that showed me the unmistakable evidence for his conclusions.

Suddenly, as he stooped over a track, the thump of fleeting hoof drifted from the woods above us. Hugh's reaction was instantaneous. In a second, his relaxed form became tense and purposeful. He dropped to a knee, leveling his rifle for action. A glimpse of white, fleeting and vague, was seen in the woods. A ram bounded to a rocky ridge and paused for only a split second.

A shot rang out. This shot split the atmosphere and rolled around the towering peaks with reverberating echoes. The ram seemed to stiffen, then it sank like a plummet to the ground. It happened all too quickly for me to fathom; yet, the pang of remorse following the shot has always remained with me. One moment, it was a thing of life and beauty roaming the land; the next, a quivering body on the ground with a trickle of blood oozing from its head. The primitive in me overcame the veneer, however, and I watched the jubilant Hugh quarter the animal. Such an easy killing was far more than he had dared to hope for, and he did not resent the fact that he, by his prowess with the rifle, had saved himself a long and perhaps fruitless day's tramp over the mountains.

"Don't hav to eat corn mush for supper tanoight!" Hugh remarked as he wiped the perspiration from his forehead. He washed his hands in the brook, gave a sigh of relief, and added, "Now, let's hev a breathin spell 'fore we lug the critter back." He made his way toward an immense boulder that stood stark against the hazy blue sky. We climbed upon it, and as I gazed around I could feel that old familiar tingle of elation that seems to surge in my veins each time I think of the magnificence of the mountain country that surrounded me. Could it be possible that these mountains had some magic power to capture the heart of everyone who roamed them? For miles, mountains rolled off to a dim horizon. Spruce forests crowned the summits, except when a rocky peak thrust its silhouette above the deep green. The lower slopes were tinged with the daubing of autumn, and the valleys were splashed with evergreens. Here and there, hidden by the forest, were lakes glistening in the sunlight. Foamy cloudlets drifted slowly across the panorama, and a hawk wheeled and dived in its flight. The beauty, the stillness, and the wildness awed me.

"Now, thet's a soight, ain't it?" remarked Hugh, as he pulled his hat down over his eyes to shield them from the sun. "Ye see thet mountain yonder? Wal, how far is it? Ten miles? Heh, heh—it's twenty."

The warm sun cast a spell of indolence over me. The whole immense world seemed to be soaking up the hot rays. A strange new stillness wrapped the peaks, and we heard a cricket. Probably because many of the impressions were entirely new, many of the minute details of that trip have remained with me.

"How much land do you own?" I queried of Hugh, for I was anxious to know just how important a man he was. I had yet to know mountain philosophy, yet to know real values.

"Wal, now, thet's kinder a sticker! Mebby I kin give ye an idee though!" Hugh replied. He pointed to a far away peak in the hazy distance and added, "See thet there knobby peak off yonder?" When I nodded that I did see it, he continued, "An ye see thet valley off thar? And, kin ye see thet pinnacle of old Eleventh?"

"But I wanted to know how much land YOU own," I answered.

A hearty laugh broke the stillness. He replied, "Why I own ALL of thet, and more, too! The sky is mine too!" He paused, then added seriously, "Thet ain't sayin' that ye don't own it just as much though."

Johnny Morehouse
My friend Johnny, philosopher. Photograph by Bill Glinesing.

Mountain philosophy! Here was a man, I later learned, who owned no earthly possessions, to say nothing of an acre of ground; yet, he was as rich as Whitney and not burdened in the least by his estate! His rule of life is to evade as much of the unpleasantness that is created by work as is possible and to enjoy as much and as many good times as possible. He further believes in completely disregarding schedules or anything suggestive of routine. The fact that he lives and enjoys good health today is proof sufficient that the idea has worked for him.

Mountain atmosphere is conducive to such a state. No one hurries in the backwoods country. There are no crowds rushing to punch a time clock, no locomotives to roar and pound the spirit of speed into one's being, and no whistles to tell one it is time to go to work. Routine is a thing almost unknown to the true Adirondack native, unless it be taken as "sugar season," or "fishin' or huntin' season."

Perhaps, this spirit is a natural reaction to the heartbreaking work of their earlier lives in subduing the wilderness. Too, many of the philosophic whitebeards of today were schooled in lumber camps, where the hours often were dawn to dusk of the hardest kind of labor. Lifelong intimacies with raw nature have embedded in the man a spirit tinged with something easy to see and feel, yet hard to understand.

The most thrifty of these people have a leaning toward the pleasures of the rod and gun. It is not uncommon for one to inquire for the master of a house at successive shacks on a warm July day only to be greeted with, "Oh, yes, he's gone fishin' too!" This life is certainly a very essential part of their existence.

• • •

No man could typify the spirit of the Adirondacks more surely than John Morehouse, the bearded patriarch of Echo Valley. His house is a short distance from my cabin. He lives an industrious life there, tilling the rocky, discouraging soil so that his wife and sturdy son, Eugene, may be comfortable. One

Johnny Morehouse's Home

glimpse of his honest, frank features is enough to see in him a character tinged with the noble. His dark blue eyes twinkle from a depth of bushy white hair. His curly hair surmounts large, well-formed features. Broad shoulders, a deep chest, and a thick bull-like neck support the fact that once he was a commanding man among hard, two-fisted men. With no small amount of pride, he tells of the days when he could throw any man in the Oregon country. Tradition has it that he could trim the finest axeman in the lumber country. Such accomplishments tell of muscle and sinew far more than mere words, for the Adirondack lumber camps harbored a brand of men known throughout the country for their strength.

Time, in its relentless way, has softened his tawny muscles, has weakened his sinewy hands, and has taken a bit of the keenness from this woodsman's eyes. According to his "cal'ation," he must be well past his seventies. Years ago, he was about sixty-five! Who knows? I have often thought that the Fountain of Youth may be found in those rugged northern hills.

Johnny Morehouse with Friends

Johnny Morehouse woke early, fed and brushed his horse, harnessed his horse to the jumper, and came with his friend Willie Keeler. They stopped in front of my cabin and shouted, "Let's go huntin', m'boy!" I always appreciated Johnny's concern for my well being and how much he included me in his activities.

John can neither read or write and says that he just "niver keered about book larnin'," but the hills have told this silent, thoughtful man many secrets about life that the scholar may never learn. The ways of the wild are an open book to him. The forest, still vast and interesting, is no longer a mystery. I think he has a compass in his brain, so surely can he traverse the pathless wilderness. I have seen him start for a tiny beaver meadow, miles over the mountain, and strike it without hesitancy or loss of time. A better companion in the woods or a keener comrade of the chase, I have never known.

"Guess I'm gittin' old, me boy," he remarked to me on a cold, rainy afternoon in early November. We stood atop a cliff brink overlooking Second Pond and were about to add *finis* to a five-day unsuccessful deer and bear hunt. Somehow, luck seemed against us on this trip. I had several good chances for a set of antlers but had missed them. John had none. Already, twilight was beginning to shroud the country. I thought I caught a glisten in the deep blue eyes of my companion, who stood lost in thought on the pinnacle, with his rifle slung easily in his arms. "H-m-m, leg weary, after only five days o' huntin', an nary a buck ta show fer it! First toime the country iver beat me, I guess!" he muttered. Then, with a wistful tone in his voice, he added, "I'm gittin' old!"

I could hardly answer, for I knew how these words hurt the pride of this man of the forests. "Ye gods!" I finally blurted out, "Who wouldn't be leg weary after the way we've been scrambling over these mountains. It's not your fault we have lost! I've had a peach of a time, regardless! Now, let's work along that ridge to camp, huh? We have to pack up yet tonight."

We started. Carefully, we still hunted the beechnut timber. Suddenly, a buck crashed out of the brush ahead of me several hundred feet away. I drew up but too late. The deer headed up the ridge toward my companion. There was a breathless interlude. Would the woodsman see? Would he shoot? Could he hit the deer in this eerie light?

I jumped as two shots smote the stillness in rapid succession. There was stillness again. Then, three, deep, houndlike bays, clear as a bell, drifted down the ridge. A lump came to my throat as the mellow notes reverberated around the peaks. Excited clear through, I hurried up the ridge and soon saw John looking dejectedly down the dense mountainside. He was a picture of melancholy.

"Guess I'm gittin' old. Only fifteen rod away and broadside—and I think I missed," John said discouragingly.

Already, dusk was falling. "How on earth did you expect to hit him in this light? Let's go over and see his tracks just for the fun of it," I said. We made our way to where the upturned leaves told the story. Stooping low, I could see a faint sign of blood. Trailing the blood about a hundred feet, I came to a small cliff. The tracks disappeared over it! I told the mountaineer to wait atop the cliff while I dashed madly around its base. At its foot, stretched full length, lay a buck. I glanced at the cliff brink. John stood there, his shoulders bent a bit, quietly silhouetted against the drab sky. "John, you old son-of-a-gun! You're sure getting old!" I yelled.

Then, I saw the old woodsman start. His head lifted, his body straightened, and a muffled exclamation escaped his lips. Lo! He was a stripling again! At least, anyone who could have seen him gut the animal, sling part of it over his shoulder, and stalk joyously down the mountain to camp would have thought as much. Anyone hearing that night, as he told stories while we roasted choice steaks over the fire, would have thought that he had recaptured his youth again.

About midnight he was finishing up another of his famous panther stories, and he seemed to be just filled with energy while I was so tired, just dead tired. "John," I said to him earnestly, "Now, I know you're not getting old." Then we crawled into our crude log hut and were lulled to sleep by the hoot of an owl on a nearby mountainside.

One of the most colorful things about John is his voice. He speaks slow and forcefully. To hear him bay like a hound on the chase, as he clambers around the jagged peaks after deer, certainly fascinates me. It is the imitation of an old fox-hound. It is clear, long, drawn out, and bell-like when you hear it on a crisp autumn morning. It echoes, mellowing the original, and catches the spirit of the great open spaces. His imitation of the owl is none other than perfect. Once, in the twilight he was atop of a ridge, and I was to come at the owl signal. About the same time that he started to signal to me, a great barred owl began to call on another nearby ridge. The call of the guide, drifting from a distance, seemed truer to me than the rightful owner of the voice.

Mountain patience is a thing of awe to most of us who are used to modern ideas. I doubt very much if there is a single acre plot of what a southern farmer would call "flat land" in the section that John is a part of. He plows and plants boulder-strewn slopes. Along with this, the soil is poor and extremely

Story Time

In the early days, I occasionally spent a week alone in the cabin, either in the fall or midwinter. Johnny was always a welcome guest, but he never came near the cabin when he could hear the sound of my fiddle drifting across the fields to his home. "I knowed you wuz happy then," he said.

Some evenings, Cabin Country would be immersed in a quiet that seemed to hang over the land. Only the hoot of an owl on the mountain would break the stillness. Then, Johnny would come over, and we would sit before the blazing fireplace as he related stories of his life. He had been a lumberjack, hunter, trapper, and guide. In those days, wolves were still there, and on rare occasions a panther. His descriptions of their habits convinced me that he spoke the truth about these animals, which later became extinct in the Adirondacks.

At times, we would just sit there, occasionally throwing another log in the fire, and plan trips back o'yonder.

Out of this friendship came visits by Johnny to my home in Niskayuna. On his first visit, I took him in late afternoon to the top of Putnam Hill, west of Schenectady, which overlooks the city.

As it got darker, the lights of the city began to come on. To his unbelieving eyes, soon the whole valley was alight.

"When do they shet them off?," he inquired. "When the sun comes up," I replied. All he could say was his favorite expression of surprise, "Judas priest!"

thin and quite some distance from his home. Yet, year after year, he grows his "'beggies'" there.

One day, I was helping him till the soil, and it was mighty hard work and very discouraging. About mid-afternoon we sat down to rest and began our usual talk about anything and everything in general. It was not surprising that we talked occasionally about the "Better Land" that we often think we will someday journey on to.

"Jist what is your idee t'other shore is lak?" he asked me seriously.

"Well, ever since I came up in this country, I kinda thought it must be something like this," I said. I gave the mountain land at our feet a wide sweep with my hand.

"Thar! Don't it beat all?" he replied after some thought. "Lots of toimes I git ta thinkin' ef I could have a hundred flat acres of land ta till, why I wouldn't keer how almighty hard the Boss made me work! Thet would be my idee of a foine place."

But that is not his general idea, for despite the fact that he must scratch and scrape from dawn to dusk to eke out a bare living, he loves his homeland. He has often told me so. "Pshaw," he says, "I jist couldn't leave this here country. Even those blasted rocks seem so friendly at toimes!"

John has one great failing—or is it a beautiful weakness? He cannot say no! He is too generous and too kindly for his own good. One winter evening, I sat with him before the roaring stove in his home. It was bitter cold outside and the stuffy heat, I must admit, felt very good. There was a commotion outside, the door suddenly opened, and in came a heavily bearded mountaineer. He shook the snow from himself, bid us the time of day, and huddled near the stove. He was a former dweller of Echo Valley. He remarked that it was cold outside and shortly took off a fur coat and threw it over a pair of antlers on the wall. At this time, he began to sing that old song, "For Anyplace I Hang My Hat Is Home Enough for Me."

With true mountain hospitality, Maude, John's wife got together a supper for their guest, who, by this time, was making himself very much at home. He said, "Thought I'd pay ye a lettle visit, jist till spring, or so. Whar did ye say I was to sleep?"

I looked at John in amazement. From the look in his eyes, I could see that his visitor was far from welcome. Truly, John was in hard straights himself. Here was a man, able-bodied, only middle aged, and generally disliked for very good reasons, that was practically forcing himself on another man much older than he. What few provisions poor John had were only by the dint of hard work. A look came into John's eyes that I could read well, and I knew that he could not tell the man that he was not wanted. "Mebby," he confided to me later, "I kin make him earn his vittles here. Can't ye see, he's harder hit thin even me?"

Frankly, I couldn't see this, and I told him so. I had to marvel at the heart that would actually halve his last crust with a practical stranger. This man stayed at John's place for nearly two months, doing a few odd chores in return for his lodging.

Outfoxed

I often roamed the hills above my cabin in the quiet peaceful afternoons and twilight hours. I knew that many animals, both large and small, dwelt on the slopes adjacent to the wilderness and gave charm to them. One of those inhabitants was a red fox.

A gorgeous September sun was painting the west with crimson and gold. Shadows were lengthening, and a fragrant breeze drifted out of the forest. I felt hugely content with the world as I stood on a boulder on Wildcat Crest. Far above, a hawk wheeled in flight. Rolling off to the distant horizon to the east and southeast were mountains, hills, and valleys. Soon, I would be going home to school, where I would recount my many adventures to my chums who knew of no such life as I was experiencing.

A clap of thunder could not have startled me more than the sharp warning whistle of a woodchuck somewhere below me. Strange, I thought, that he would whistle without cause, for surely he had not seen me. I leapt off the rock and crawled to the edge of the knoll and peered over.

A flash of fur glided past me, and I saw that it was a red fox. With a few bounds he reached the crest of the hill. Silhouetted against the sky, he ran nose high, tail flying jauntily, the personification of grace, beauty, and speed. In a trice, he was gone as quickly as he had come. I had forgotten my rifle, which lay next to me, my wits, everything—except the sense of awe at the picture he had presented. Then a feeling of remorse came over me thinking of the glory that would have been mine as I stood surrounded by my chums in the city and told the story of the fall of that red roamer. Why hadn't I shot? Why?

As I walked down the old sheep trail to my cabin that evening, I made a firm resolve. I would have that red pelt if I never did another thing.

Day after day, week after week, all the next summer I roamed the hills. I saw foxes, shot at them, and missed. It seemed the sense of awe I knew with each succeeding glimpse completely overshadowed the grim determination to satisfy the urge to kill. Once as I lay behind a boulder watching for "chucks," a fox walked to within fifty feet of me and stopped. He lay down, rolled over such as a dog often does, got up, and shook his glistening red coat. He sniffed the air, seemed undecided as just what to do, and sat down to contemplate whether he would prefer a fat partridge or one of the mountaineer's dwindling flock of hens.

"Shoot, man shoot!" I said to myself, finally realizing that the much coveted pelt sat less than fifty feet away. I shot! Anyone would have wondered how I could have missed him.

I think that the snows have told me more intimate secrets of Reynard's life than all other observations put together. Day after day, I have followed his straight, catlike tracks in the valley, in the swamps, and around the lonely peaks. Many times I have come upon the remains of the partridge, the hare, and the other wood folk, victims of his version of the law of the wild. Few winter sports are so absorbing.

Mountaineers attribute weird doings to this elusive hill-lover. He will uncover their carefully concealed traps, fool the most sagacious foxhound, work ructions with flocks of prized hens, and no matter how persistently hunted, will continue to leave his trademarks around the cabins at night. He seems to be almost reckless at times. Endowed with a fine sense of real courage, he seldom lets this get beyond his real judgment. Only once do I recall an apparent lack of good sense on his part.

Near Diamond Mountain, there is a deep gully. A great hemlock, uprooted by the storms, had fallen and bridged the gap. Snow and ice covered the upper side of the tree, making a crest of about two inches on the entire length of this span. A fox I had trailed for miles in a light fluffy snow had not even hesitated before crossing this precarious bridge, if my ability to read tracks is fair. Observing the jagged rocks below where he would have landed had he fallen, it seemed to me that death might have claimed him for a single misstep on the snow-covered ice on the tree. Perhaps he figured that quickness of body would save him. Because he was not pressed by hounds or men, it seems to be more probable that he simply knew he was not going to fall. This was just a casual incident in his life.

Night in the Wilderness

W ho-hooa-who who." A great gray shadow drifted over
our campfire and was lost in the blackness of some
spruces. Drifting on the wings of a gentle west wind came the
plaintive song of a fox. From the northern shore of Lost Lake,
the mighty precipices of a mountain rose sheer into moonlit
turquoise, alive with hordes of the stars. From a hidden glen
came the tinkle of a waterfall, restless waves lapped seethingly
on rugged shores, an occasional whisper came from the evergreens, the sages of an almost forgotten country.

"It's callin', me b'y, let's go!" Through the bluish smoke
of the dying fire I caught a look of anticipation steal over the
bronzed, weatherbeaten face of my companion. He stirred the
embers, put another birch log on the fire, and arose. His six
feet of sinew and muscle towered above me. Adjusting his
slouch hat, he grabbed a paddle, and both of us went to the
boat.

"Just what is this that calls each night, Jim?"

"Don't know," he chuckled. "Less'n it's the night itself!"

In a trice, we had left our island camp and were skimming
across the shimmering waters. Driven by my companion's prac-
ticed muscles, the little craft seemed a thing of life. He worked
it along the shoreline, dipping into cove and bayou as easily
and as silently as a wraith shadow. He seemed to know precisely where each game trail led from the dense weeds to the
water.

27

Drifting into a ghostly secluded cove, Jim brought the craft to a halt, just as its bottom eased against a submerged log. Being in the bow with a flashlight, I was ready and tense for the whisper of my companion. "Now, ter yer reight!"

A large mother coon and three youngsters looked into the prying beam. The elder turned her head from side to side, an amusing expression on her beautiful face. The youngsters were not so calm. There was a low whicker, and they scurried into the shadows. A moment later the elder followed, not without a look of maternal self-assurance. She probably decided it was better fishing further up the lake.

With a muffled exclamation of "Thar! Warn't thet purty?" Jim paddled out of the cove and up along the shore toward the head of the lake. Seldom did our nocturnal trips fail to take us into one of the most fascinating spots I have ever seen. It takes skill to guide a boat to the inlet, for one must know where the shallow sandbars, the hidden rocks, and floating islands are. Yet without a single grating sound, we reached the break, the inlet.

East Brook is a deep, languid stream fed by springs of the mountain. It issues from the heart of a dense tamarack swamp there. Thick alders line its twisting course. Towering, moss-covered tamaracks arch the limpid water. Occasionally, a game trail makes a break in the alders, and at such places one can see for some distance into the swamp.

No place could be more wildly beautiful, nor more strongly suggestive of some ancient scene. Everywhere is thick, velvety moss. It makes even mounds of harsh stumps; it enfolds fallen trees; it clings eagerly to the lower trunk of every tree. Lacelike leaves of the tamarack droop gracefully from the branches. When moon rays slant through the thick foliage the predominating green seems to take a weird luster against purplish shadows. All of this is tempered by silence only wild creatures break.

With never a betraying splash to mar the eerie stillness, my companion had worked the craft for some distance up the stream. Coming to a dark pool that marked a bend, we stopped. A faint splash came to my ears.

"Thar! Ahid e' ye! Yer leight!" An excited whisper came to me, a hand touched my shoulder, and Jim pointed upstream. Nervously, I fumbled with the light and flashed it on. Not twenty feet away, standing knee deep in water, was a magnificent buck, drinking. In a flash his antlered head came up and two green coals gazed wildly at us. For a second, he stood as a statue, alert, tensed, yet calm in this possible danger. The real spirit of the wild could hardly be more clearly exemplified. It caught me so suddenly that I dropped the light, and a tremendous splash broke the water aside me. A vague fear gripped me. There was an ungodly snort, the glimpse of a large body hurtling through the air, and a crash. A few thumps in the depths of the swamp—and stillness again.

"Heh'heh'heh! Ye blasted old bruiser! See yuh next month on the hard'ood ridge. An' moind, don't ye ferget!" With a few more such expletives, the mountaineer turned our craft and headed to the lake again. Once there, he struck for the middle, heading for an immense lone pine on a silvered island where the feeble glow of a smoldering campfire sent its beckoning glow to two of its lovers.

Many such evenings are mine, evenings entirely filled with adventure and with comradeship of true men of the mountains. Jim enriched me with the lore of a lifetime spent within the heart of nature. Some of the insignificant details of our adventures remain indelibly with me. Jim, the unassuming mountaineer, slaked my boyhood thirst for adventure, changed a vague fear of wilderness nighttime into an intense love for the shadowland.

•   •   •

Night is a continuous succession of harmonies, soft and incomparable. When twilight falls with its mellow hush, gray shadows melt into the black. Spruce clad peaks blend into the turquoise sky. Moonbeams soften the more gaudy colors. Trees whisper. Insects rasp. Peepers send their monotone from the swamps. Some harmonies are more complete than others. I have often found myself breathless at the delicateness, the exquisiteness, of some particular setting.

It is hard for me to divine a greater contentment than to wander slowly along a forgotten mountain trail after sunset. I have learned more about the life of wild creatures then than at any other time, for darkness is to them what day is to man. Nature concentrates her activities in those hours between dusk and dawn.

Positive magnificence, awesome majesty, a sense of the mysterious—we feel these when we walk beneath the Milky Way. Nothing is harsh or artificial about night. We like the mystical, the unreal. The most common tree has an individual charm when drenched with moonlight or shadows. The most ordinary hillside takes upon it an air of solemnity. The stars have a way of making us feel intimate with all creation. Beneath them we have heard, at rare intervals, that indescribable melody of silence.

At no other time are we reminded of our positive insignificance as we are at night. Creation takes upon itself a bigness seldom felt in the sunlight. Our senses clear themselves of the fogs of self-interest and become alive with wonderment. The inarticulate self, surrounded by the splendors that are not the work of man, gravitates to new levels. In turn, we feel a very real intimacy with all that is—the earth, the sky, the mountains, the lakes, the untamed inhabitants of them all—and with our fellow men. We are able to divorce ourselves from petty things; and in doing just that, we are able to judge the real values of life more accurately.

• • •

A campfire leaps into a wilderness blackness, grotesque shadows play in fantasy upon the trees and dance upon a starlit water. A hidden waterfall rumbles into the air. Through the swaying branches of a forest giant, we catch the profile of a mountain, its ragged crags in bold relief against the sky. A loon wails demonically at the stillness. An owl's call is mockingly reverberated by the cliffs. A muffled cry, a splashing of water, mysterious silence again. A vagrant breeze fans the embers of my fire and memory.

The Old Log Cabin

Winter in Cabin Country
Photograph by Gertrude Fogarty.

The first time I laid eyes on this old log cabin I fell in love with it. It was situated in a highland meadow that reached to a brook at the foot of a precipitous mountain. A main trail into a vast mysterious wilderness passed its door. It was owned by our mountaineer friend Johnny Morehouse. A combination of family encouragement and the saving of a few dollars from our apprentice courses made it possible for my brother Vincent and me to purchase it in 1926.

It was a simple structure of adz-hewn logs, eight or twelve inches in diameter. Though its logs were weathered by nearly a century of storms and its roof layered patch upon patch, it became our pride and joy at once. It had but two rooms, one with a table, chairs, and a wood stove, and the other with bunks. As we were able, we added a fireplace and then a well with a sweep, rope, and pail to lift the cold, nectarlike water from its depths.

Possession of this Adirondack pioneer's cabin quickly changed my life. My friends from the city now had a place with free lodging in a vast wild region where they could hunt deer and bear and fish for trout. And I had, without cost, free transportation almost whenever I wanted it, in rather ancient open touring cars in which we nearly froze when it got cold.

As we began to use the cabin, the whole country began to challenge us. We found streams and lakes abundant with trout and trails with fresh tracks of deer and bear. The nearby mountains were trail-less and exceeded three thousand feet in height. We soon were standing on storm swept peaks looking out to distant horizons. On one mountain, we discovered five streams, one of which was fed by a great swamp and spawned a cataract a thousand feet high.

From the cabin, as well as from all nearby clearings, the graceful Crane Mountain dominated the view. It invited exploration. Several very steep trails rose from the historic Elliot Putnam farm, located three miles back in the woods. They led to a glacial lake in a bowl below its summit and to the forest ranger's observatory. From its isolated peak, we could see most of the Adirondacks, some of the Catskills, and part of the Green Mountains of Vermont. On a rocky rampart of the mountain, we could see our Cabin Country and the vast wilderness beyond it.

Hunting and fishing became a part of our life. I was lucky to have gotten an antlered buck and a bear by the time I was seventeen, but many of my friends were not so successful. In fact many of our hunts were magnificently unsuccessful. Time and again we would hunt mountains, ridges, and swamps from dawn to dusk and come back to the cabin and eat pork and beans. At such times, the memory of the taste of fresh venison and its fragrant cooking odor would renew in us the spirit of the chase. Always, there would be a tomorrow when the buck we missed had larger antlers. We were more successful trout fishing. For this most beautiful of all fish was to be found in every stream, in or out of the wilderness, and in all of the lakes we knew but one.

During my apprenticeship as a carpenter, my boss would let me have time off as fall crept into winter and outdoor work became more difficult. One year, he let me take a month off to work with a skilled taxidermist. Usually, I would spend a week during the winter at the cabin. Most of the time I would be alone, but once in a while I would invite a fellow hitchhiker I had met on my journey north to join me. To encourage drivers of cars to pick me up, I always had traps visible in the top of my pack on the way north and a batch of tanned furs visible on the way south.

Sometimes when bitter cold permeated the logs or their interstices, I questioned my sanity. Less than eighty miles distant was a warm home and wonderful meals cooked by my

The Old Log Cabin

mother. At such times, I would throw another log on the fire, get out my fiddle, and try to make music like old Hugh Lackey.

Those winter days were priceless to me, for I had a haven where I could immerse myself in cooking and read without disturbance. I brought along books by John Burroughs, Henry David Thoreau, Francis of Assisi, and Viscount François René de Chateaubriand. Verplanck Colvin's descriptions of some of the country back and beyond kept inspiring me to know the country better. It was in this hermitage that I began to think about writing. It began in the dim light of an oil lamp and the occasional flare-ups of a dry log in the fireplace. Some of those early stories are included in this section of the book.

Winter Night Companions

It was a bitter winter night. The wind fairly shrieked around my cabin, piling snow high against the weatherbeaten logs. Occasionally, there was a lull in the storm, and the stillness in the cabin seemed to intensify. Then with what seemed to be renewed fury, the winds lashed my haven again, weird and diabolical.

I blessed the whiskered mountaineer who had advised against my taking a proposed snowshoe trip overnight into Second Pond. "The signs," he had counseled me that morning, "jist ain't roight. Better wait till termorrer, m' boy." My cabin was comfortable, decidedly so. A cheery fire in the fireplace sent shadows flickering around the room. Dry split hardwood was stacked high. I settled into a favorite old rocker. With the merry crackle of wood to add to the coziness, the aromatic smell of baking beans to temper the air, and a sense of security from the elements to make me hugely content, I was ready for a long quiet evening with my dreams. The thought that adventure might be found within the walls of such a hermitage never occurred to me. Adventure had always been synonymous with strenuous mountain climbing or trailing a deer or bear or other animals inhabiting the vast country around me.

Quite suddenly, I saw a little blackish form dash across one of the logs over the table. It stopped when it came to a tree fungus that I had nailed on the wall for use as a shelf. Subconsciously, I looked for a stick or something that I could hurl at the intruder, one of those exasperating deer mice that had an uncanny knowledge of how to do the most possible damage to my food supplies. Several times recently, they had pillaged my stores, wrecked havoc with bread I had so painstakingly baked in a reflector oven, and gnawed holes in a box of raisins.

"Eek-eek." A second mouse scurried along a higher log and with a leap too quick for my eye to follow jumped to the fungus beside my first visitor. Their beady eyes surveyed everything about the room. I lay aside the block of kindling I had picked up and shifted a bit in my chair so as to observe them better.

Evidently, they were carrying on a conversation of some sort. I remember wishing that I had the ears to get the drift of their lingo. I fancied a bit of it.

"Well, Jake, what's on the program tonight? Any cookies we might get into?" I imagined the other one replying, "The tightwad. Why he even put that hardtack in the tin, but listen . . . " Then I imagined the two outlaws planning their escapades in quest of food. They stood there, their beady eyes roving but watchful of their persecutor reclining in the chair by the fire. Then, with a dash they ran along the logs to the cupboard. They scrambled over the dishes and pan in their search for a meal.

It was hard to feel other than friendly toward even such rodents as mice on such an evening. Five minutes before I had felt distinctly alone on the edge of the wilderness, but now here I was with two companions. Companions? The thought struck me as being ludicrous; but even though they were just mice, I decided to see if I could cultivate a little intimacy with them. Certainly, I could spare enough food to supply two little mice and not begrudge the fact!

A little later, they were back on the fungus again. For the first time in my life, I saw a singular beauty in the little brown bodies. Their coats were sleek and glossy. In their eyes, there seemed to be a sparkle of mischief and adventure. Their large ears, like a deer's, were constantly moving. They were gracefully plump, and I thought again about the bread they had gotten into.

Life! It was there on the fungus, just as certain as it was in the deer and bear! Because they were small, was life less sweet to them than to the great buck bounding through the forest? Was it less real, less absorbing? Think of the immensity of their home. Dozens and dozens of square feet under the cabin with countless nooks and corners, dark passageways, great clusters of hay in the bunks. These were just a few of the things that made up their home. Just think of all the dusty beams they had to explore.

I decided to pay no attention to them, hoping that such indifference might make them less afraid of me. They continued to survey me. There remained a look of curiosity in their beady eyes, or was it my imagination running wild? Perhaps the shadows of the firelight occasionally put a wrinkle on one's brow or a devilish smile on the other.

I twisted in my chair, and the movement sent them scurrying. I decided to make sure that my food was protected in tins or jars and set out some odds and ends where they could get them.

Conquest of Thunder's Nest

All we need then is bacon?"

"Yep, then rest for a few days!" My comrade yawned. "Oh, man!"

I left him musing before the cheery blaze in the great stone fireplace in our log cabin, stepped into the night, strapped on snowshoes, and started down the mountain to Baker's Mills, a quaint little village in the valley two miles away. It was winter, 1930.

The air was keen, the snows deep. No stars were visible, but the moon, surrounded with a great, pellucid halo, looked down upon the still, white world. Eight miles across the valley, Crane Mountain's massive hulk rose mightily into the dome of heaven. A beautiful, titanic thing is Crane, so aptly called *Moos-Pot-En-Wa-Cho*, or "Thunder's Nest" by the Indians. Quite suddenly, a vague unrest surged in my veins! "Come," it said, "Star me with your lone campfire!" The call was plain, to answer inevitable.

Quickening my pace, it was but a short while before I reached the general store. A group of mountaineers, true to Adirondack tradition, were lounging around the pot-bellied stove. Yarns and various "cal'lations" filled the stuffy atmosphere. There are few things more fascinating to me than to hear such a group on such a night. After a time, I inquired from them what was the best winter trail to the mountain's peak.

41

A bearded mountaineer squinted at me through bushy eyebrows. "Wal now, me b'y, thar jist haint none. Nobody keers about climbin' thet mountain in winter. Reckon not."

Such a discussion that question started! When I finally left, a number of conflicting "idees" were still going the rounds. However, a fair idea for the most probable ascent was mine. It was the Elliot Putnam trail on the southern side of the mountain.

Over a steaming bowl of soup, I unfolded my plans to my comrade. He looked at me despairingly.

"I thought you were gonna rest for a few days! Oh well, 'philosophically' more power to you!"

January 28 dawned gray. It was snowing hard on a forty-inch blanket. Undecided, I waited. About noon it let up a bit, and I started. The day's objective was to reach Lake Clear, a supposedly "bottomless" body of water about half a mile from the peak. A lean-to would serve as shelter for the night. The round trip, being in the neighborhood of fourteen miles, bid me to pack light. Only bare necessities, plus the luxury of a camera, found their way into the pack.

Most of the snowshoeing was cross-country. It was nothing short of joy to slowly creep toward the mountain. It loomed ever more immense until, at Elliot Putnam's house, it towered steeply above me. When I finally left this hospitable hermitage, it was not without a clear idea of what I was up against. This fine, gray-eyed preacher had been turned back himself. The benefit of his experience was invaluable to me.

About three o'clock, the actual ascent began, although I had been gaining altitude steadily for the past two miles. The trail crossed a brook, raised sharply, and cut diagonally across the face of the mountain to the overflow of the lake. The climb was slow work and tedious. Mostly, it was a tree-to-tree ascent, although in many places they were sadly lacking. Ledges at several places permitted but the width of one snowshoe. Without the comparatively short "bear paw" snowshoes, more round than long, I doubt if this trail is feasible for winter climbing.

Although it was cold, about half way up, I shed my coat and sweater, packing both. This was preferable to overheating. The day was nearly spent, so it was necessary to hurry. Once after a really hard struggle up a particularly steep ledge, I flung myself to the cooling snow. A small avalanche resulted, and a moment later I was back where I'd begun some minutes before.

At last, I reached the overflow. I knew that the lake water would coat the rocks with ice; one had to be wary. Enthusiastically, I turned toward the valley wherein dwells Mr. Putnam and gave a long, houndlike bay. My heart leapt when from afar his bell-like answer came ringing back!

Scrambling over the last rocks, I saw the lake. It was a sheet of white, fringed with spruces. Just beyond its northern shoreline, a great mass of rock raised black and sober against the sky, which had suddenly cleared for the sunset to fire. The clouds tinted from crimson to old rose and gold. A last shaft of sunlight lit the rocky peak a half mile away. I hailed its majesty. "Tomorrow," I murmured, "You and I win!"

A keen breeze on my cheek warned of the fast approaching darkness. I hurried over to my anticipated home. A huge snowdrift met my searching gaze. A small hole in it belied the fact of the shelter. I peered into it. A porcupine bristled its quill a few feet in. The fact that he is no tidy housekeeper moved me to look for another place. On the eastern shore was a cabin that the ranger used to occupy. It had fallen to ruin, or nearly so, by disuse, and a smaller snowbank was in front of it.

An energetic half hour found me with an eight-foot circle dug into three feet of snow, a fire at one end, and my duffel on the other. Just after I finished cutting my first log for firewood, my hatchet broke off clean. This was misfortune, for now all of my firewood had to be dead stuff that I could break with my hands. It took over an hour to get a sizable supply.

Supper was in order. Hot tomato soup, black bread, bacon, peas, potatoes, and pears. How I lingered over that meal, watching the stars as they foamed in the gulf of heaven and the shafts of moonlight sparkle on the snow. How cheerily the campfire leapt into the night! A vagrant wind stirred the spruces overhead. Once a snowshoe rabbit hopped within the light. A domelike mass of rock crept out of the lake to form the north-western horizon. Dwarfed, mangled red pines stood bravely there to break the starkness of the rock.

After minutes of luxuriant ease beside the fire, I cleaned the dishes with snow water and prepared for the night. A fallen spruce yielded some boughs, which I put under the sleeping bag, and I covered the entire lower portion of the bag with snow. The warmth of the bag felt good, for it was fast becoming bitterly cold. To lie out there under the open sky was to feel the joy of life's cup being filled to overflowing. With mental unrest gone and weird shadows dancing fantastically on the overhanging branches, I soon knew oblivion.

It must have been midnight when I first awoke, for the moon had slipped some distance across the sky. An awful cold had somehow entered the bag and chilled me to the bone. My breath had frozen to hoar frost on the bear fur inside the bag! A few cheerless embers smoldered in the fire bed. The wind had increased, and howled, and swept sheets of snowdust on my bed. Nature had taken on a harsh and desolate cloak. As indecision swept over me, I wondered what madness had lured me to this lonely, forsaken place!

There was no alternative to getting up and moving. I soon had a blaze defiantly mocking the stars. Crouching beside the blaze, I had to marvel at the strangeness of the cold. This kind was new to me, though my winter camps had been many. Strapping on the webs, I ran across the lake to increase circulation. Then I'd pack up and leave for some warm place! It was almost bright as day out. From the farther shore, the peak was plainly visible. It was a thing of moon-drenched glory. To leave without standing atop . . . but why not climb it now? A mad thought . . . but possible. Perhaps we would somehow hold out until dawn. Perhaps.

It must have been about 1:00 A.M. when the final climb began. From the start, it assumed the nature of hard work; lack of sleep had told on me. Because of the icy crust that at times defied my efforts to dig in, the ranger's trail was discounted.

The southern side of the mountain, while steep, offered better snowshoeing. For the first time in my life, I found myself urging my webbed understandings along aloud. This phase of the trip was mostly a struggle in myself. It seemed so easy to turn back.

An eternity seemed to have passed. Who can know the joy when at last the bare rocks leading to the summit were reached? My emotion was mostly awe because of the grandeur that met every searching glance. Far, far below lay Lake Clear, heart-shaped, still as death. A hundred peaks—their sharp contours smoothed to a velvetlike evenness by a sheen of moonlight—lay before me. I ran to a last stand upon the utter pinnacle.

What an immense unreality the world was! From where I stood, the rocks dropped precipitously hundreds of feet. Garnet Lake was clearly distinguishable. It was next to impossible to look north toward the Marcy Range. The wind was too rapierlike. It stung the eyes and blurred the vision, but my blood surged! I felt puny and positively insignificant to the mighty forces of Nature—a privileged man with wondering eyes!

Once again, the cold moved me to action. Just below the summit, the ranger had an emergency shelter. It was nearly buried in snow, so I had to dig to find the door, which was partly crushed in. Inside was a stove, a bunk, and a pile of hardwood. What a multitude of blessings were showered upon the thoughtful ranger that morning! In short order, a fire was roaring up the chimney, and the stove began to glow red. Eating a bit of chocolate, I lay upon the bunk while an unceasing wind howled around the cabin. Sleep came quickly.

Just before dawn, I awoke and went to the peak again. With infinite slowness, the sky to the east lightened. It was wonderfully clear. (The ranger had told me I would be able to see 125 miles on a very clear day.) Among the ranges visible were the Catskills, the Green Mountains, and the White Mountains. The Marcy Range loomed magnificently to the north, forming a ragged, peak-studded skyline. Gore and Eleventh formed a beautiful view to the west.

To see the sky in the east change color was a most wonderful sight. A line of dark clouds slowly became tinted with delicate shades of violet, rose, and amber. I climbed to the top rung of the ranger's tower. While the steel trusses fairly hummed, I took pictures and waited for the coming of the sun.

Slowly, the great orb climbed over a far jagged range. It shot long, cometlike shafts of light to the taller peaks. They assumed strange new life. The sky became an intense blue. For long emotional minutes, I watched. Then the cold bade me to move on.

It was with a light heart and a vastly enriched sense of beauty that I started the descent. When I reached the pond, I packed up and started back. The descent to Putnam's was a joy. Places I had won with six-inch side steps now were now slid down yards at a time. In due time, I reached the preacher's house and gladly accepted the mountain hospitality he offered. As the inner man was being satisfied, we yarned long about our beloved "Thunder's Nest." Then, I again shouldered the pack and began the return. The snow was ideal, and the trip was made without accident.

Never had the cabin seemed more welcome! I was really tired and eager for warmth and balsam bunk. My comrade was jubilant, and he plied me with questions. After coffee, I went to the wonderful comforts of the bunk.

Awakening from a dreamless sleep many hours later, I ran to the window. There it loomed, the graceful Crane, in dark silhouette against a violet sky. Somehow it seemed more graceful, more beautiful, more friendly, less inanimate. Again, its inarticulate voice reached across the snows. This time it told of victory for two. I know that on some winter's day, I'll be trudging across the vast silence again and that on some winter's night my lone campfire will leap to the stars high up on Crane's alluring trail!

The Still Hunters

October dawn. The little old log cabin. Cataract Mountain sparkling with the first rays of the sun. Majestic Crane, rugged Huckleberry, and other ranges hazy with mist.

A beech fire crackling in the fireplace. Flapjacks, bacon, and coffee giving sweet aroma to the cabin. Breakfast for two.

A final inspection of favorite rifles and out into the crisp morning air, away. To the ledges and ridges of Cataract and Diamond mountains for me. To the lower hills and hardwood ridges for my friend. Deer and bear.

Deep thrilling breaths of spruce and balsam and of the wilderness. Splendid forests a riot of color. Scarlet, crimson, and gold. A brisk hike to the base of the mountain. The climb. The hunt.

Moccasined feet leave a deer trail and head into the trackless forest. Hoary moss-covered rocks. Tumbling, splashing waterfalls. Immense cliffs, jagged crags, and ledges. Rutted deer trails.

Fresh deer tracks.

A song in the heart!

Silence. The chatter of red squirrel. A blue jay scolding from a dead stub. Sunbeams piercing the leafy canopy of the trees.

Life!

The blue of the heavens. A tang in the air. A ledge and a rest. The climb again. Up. Deer upward. Mighty ranges now

Pioneers, 1921–1930

These two men were the pioneers of my life in the Adirondacks. This photograph was taken on the island in a lake in the Siamese Ponds Wilderness. My father sits in the doorway of the cabin, and my Uncle Frank Holtslag is in the tent in the foreground. This place is four miles from the clearing and is reached by a trail that winds its rough way through a forest of giant hardwoods. Photographer unknown.

clearing of mist. More fresh deer tracks. Bear sign. A laughing, tumbling cataract. A sudden flash of dun. A hasty aim. The crack of a rifle.

Thundering echoes. A crash. A miss.

Higher, ever higher on the mountain. Numerous ledges. Fresh humus over leaves just fallen. Hours of tracking.

Noontime. A tiny campfire. White smoke curling upward. Three-thousand feet above Lake Champlain in the far, misty distance. Mountains, hills, and valleys. Beauty everywhere.

The hunt again. Expectations. Anticipation. The sun beginning to tint western skies. Billowy cloud forms aglow. A

Still Hunter

fresh night wind born on the nearby summit. The first gentle shades of dusk. The hoot of an owl. The crack of a twig.

A brown form on a ledge ahead. Antlers.

The rifle shot echoes from the summit.

Silence.

A hunter descending the mountain. A shank of venison lashed to his rifle. Twilight. The first evening star. A shadowy trail. The clearing.

A light in the cabin. The door opens to a cheerful fire within. Adventures on the ridge, on the mountain, before the fireplace. Steak, potatoes, steaming coffee. Shadows flickering on the log walls. Coals growing mellow.

To bed on bunks of straw. Peace!

Wilderness Hunting Camp

Wilderness Hunting Camp in Diamond Mountain Meadow

Answering the ancient call of our hunting forbearers, our hunting party goes back into the wilderness to hunt. Now, decades later, the sons and grandsons of members of our original hunting party still set up camp each fall.

Three miles back in the woods from the cabin clearing, we hunters have known life in tents each fall for decades. Our favorite site was an ancient beaver meadow at the end of a boulder-strewn trail in the Siamese Ponds Wilderness. A crystal stream bisects the meadow and hurries several miles to a wild river near the heart of the wild country. A mountain rises precipitously a thousand feet above the site, and four cataracts flow off its north side and add their tribute to the stream.

Two 14- by 16-foot wall tents joined together are pitched at the east end of an acre of grass and sunshine. Our first state permit for such a camp at Diamond Mountain meadow was issued by a forest ranger in 1933. We camped there each year after that until the beavers came back and reclaimed the meadow twenty-seven years later. Then, we moved downstream to a little clearing aside a cataract, high enough to avoid such disturbance again. We continue to camp here.

This part of the wilderness is wild and precipitous. Mechanized vehicles have been left far behind. Ancient hardwoods dominate the forest. Spruce and balsam line the waters and are etched against the skyline on mountaintops. From our tents, sunsets, often of crimson and burnished gold, light the narrow valley between the mountains to the west. Some nights, the stars hang like lanterns in a black velvet sky. And on others, moonlight drenches the land and sparkles on running streams.

It is ideal country for the white-tailed deer and black bear, creatures of almost unbelievable sagacity and grace. They know how to take advantage of every cliff, thicket, and swamp. In our country, they bed on ledges high on the north side of the mountain from where they can see extensively down the mountain through the woods. They are endowed with radar to add to their sensitive hearing. On high mountains with evergreens and swamps, they are almost impossible to get. In such places, the heavy-antlered bucks live almost unmolested because of the special attributes they possess. Only when they leave the high country for short periods in the fall are they in danger from man. From long experience, we find success on the lower hills and upland swamps in late November.

The challenge to get a trophy buck in country as wild as this is so compelling that it brings hunters back to the remote areas year after year whether they are successful or not. And the essence of an Adirondack wilderness hunting camp is much more than the success of the hunt. Rather, it is the adventure in a land untamed by man. It is experiences in a land that has been saved from vanishing, so rarely the case across the landscape of America.

Hunting season is late October and November for six to ten companions from all walks of life. Summer has fled, and most tourists have left the mountains. The leaves of the hardwoods, so recently a riot of color, now cover the forest floor. The days get progressively shorter and colder. The weather is unpredictable. A first dusting of snow comes early to our camp, which is nearly two thousand feet above Lake Champlain. The first snow sometimes is followed by a heavy storm that nearly flattens our tents. On occasion, thunder echoes between the peaks in narrow valleys, and lightning seems more fearsome than we have witnessed when inside our comfortable homes. Torrents of rain sometimes transforms streams into rivers. Sleet often follows. Ice skims the beaver ponds, and we can trace the animals route from his lodge to his pantry of bark on the bottom of the pond below the thick ice by the air holes he keeps open. The cold creates fantasies of ice crystals on splashing cataracts. One small stream above camp, dropping its water on a flat boulder, forms round ice balls about three-quarters of an inch in diameter.

Into this wild country, our hunters make their home for several weeks or more each year. The native mountain teamster makes such living possible by hauling in our heavy equipment for the period involved. Our present teamster has performed this task for eighteen years, not only for us but for many similar groups with camps in remote regions of this wilderness. This kind of experience recalls the traditional days of hunting in years long gone by—a tradition almost forgotten in this mechanized age.

Especially memorable to all of us have been those days when guides and mountaineers from Cabin Country have joined us in the hunt and in camp. Each of them has in his repertoire tales of early days and pioneer experiences. They always are the life of the party. We respect their sense of independence and often marvel at their ability to improvise craftsmanship with materials that simply should not work—like replacing babbitt in a piston of a car with canvas.

Days in camp begin with a hearty breakfast of fruit, bacon, eggs, flapjacks, and coffee. Then it's off to the places we envision our quarry likely to be. Wherever that might be, in our country, it means climbing—a hardwood ridge, a cliff, or a mountain. Level ground is rare. Our hunt is seeking the wild places and the signs of animals we have seen. It is reaching, out-of-breath, a ledge atop cliffs from which we can see a wonderful profusion of country stretching to a far horizon.

We become acutely conscious of wood folk. Flights of chickadees, the chatter of squirrels, a grouse startling us as it bursts out ahead of us. Pileated woodpeckers drumming on a hollow tree. A three-toed woodpecker backing down a spruce. Light snow reveals the travels of a coyote, fox, and snowshoe rabbit. Bear tracks are rare but add excitement to the day. We also occasionally find the empty skin of a porcupine that served as a dinner for a fisher. And once in a great while, someone sees a bobcat.

We begin to feel once again that we are part of this country. We find a well-used deer crossing above the high falls of a cataract. We come upon a recently used bear wallow in the depths of a swamp. We find a hidden vale, where the earth is trampled with the hooves of bucks challenging each other. There is an infinity of natural wonders all around us.

Methods of hunting are as varied as the hunters themselves. Weather is a predominant factor. Noisy leaves underfoot, the silence of walking on fresh snow, the direction of the wind, and the temperature all are factors in where we go and with whom. We become very sensitive to the elements, even as do the deer and bear.

The hunter's objective is to outwit his quarry. A very high percentage of the time, it is the hunter who is outwitted. More times than not, our most careful and exhaustive actions are nullified by the marvelous sensibilities of the animals. And often, because of the extent of the wilderness, a deer avoiding a hunter moves in directions where he may not be bothered again by anyone of the human species until another year.

The highlight of the usual hunting day is lunchtime around a blazing campfire, where we recall the experiences of the morning. Usually, they are along some stream or by a beaver pond, a mile or more from the tents and well above them in elevation.

The country around us dominates our thoughts. Everywhere are mountains, forests, gullies, and cliffs. We may hear an occasional hunter in some far distance, but we seldom see anyone except our companions. Just to see deer and watch them fade like shadows into the woods is exciting. To be so frequently outwitted by them is the reason why hunting in wilderness is so challenging.

Occasionally, success crowns our efforts. Then the hard work begins. To get the antlered buck to camp often requires dragging him for miles, over mountains, down cliffs, across streams, and around beaver ponds. When at last we reach the open hardwoods above camp, we begin to sense the fulfillment of an ancient call.

Camp life at such times is the only joy we want to know. The warmth of the tent, the companionship of our friends, the wonderful hours lingering over a memorable meal in the dim light and shadows of lanterns—these are moments to be treasured forever. Here we recount the adventures of other years and hilarious times. Here the philosophical exploration of each other's hopes and dreams tell the hours away until the fire dies down and sleeping bags invite us to think about our unique experiences.

When the hunt is over, and tents and equipment are made ready for our teamster, we know that another fine chapter in our lives is being completed. There will be, we hope, another such year. We also know that innumerable times in the coming year, when beset with the problems we all face, we will be recalling those splendid hours and the words of Robert W. Service: "There's the land, oh, it beckons and beckons,

And I want to go back and I will!"

The Lure of the Hunt

When I was seventeen, I heard in my subconscious the clarion call of my forbearers—the hunters—to kill a bear. I dreamed of it and never questioned that it would be fulfilled, especially because the year before I had taken an antlered buck.

I felt it quite natural when my father asked me to help guide a group of his old Albany cronies on a three-day deer hunt in Cabin Country. One fine October day, six of his friends came to his camp. For most of them, including my father, this was to be their first hunt. Dad had asked our neighbor John Dalaba to guide, and I was to assist. John was a tall, blue-eyed, soft-spoken mountain man and a good hunter.

Early the next morning, we headed up the Second Pond trail and in about an hour we were at Bog Meadow in Mud Pond country. About noon, we had lunch on a big rock near the outlet of the pond. Our chances for success were discussed. George Deiseroth, who had retired and moved to the north country years before, summed up our thoughts just before we left for the next drive when he said, "Pick up some of those beech nuts and get a pocketful of deer tracks, and we'll stew 'em tonight."

On the second morning, John suggested that we hunt Hardwood Ridge, a somewhat less strenuous hike than that of the previous day. And he said with a smile, "It's as likely a place not to see deer as anywhere I can take you."

My Father's Hunting Party

This group of hunters were friends of my father's from Albany. The only individuals who had hunted big game before were the two men kneeling and the man second from the right, George Deiseroth, a retired baker from Albany who lived in Cabin Country. My father is on the right. Second from the left is John Dalaba, a wonderful mountain man whose son-in-law, Earl Allen, is now teamster for our wilderness camp.

So we again headed up the trail. John had me take the group down along Diamond Mountain Brook trail about a mile. I was to place the men up the ridge, and then I would go to the top of the ridge. John would drive westerly along the top until he reached me.

When I reached the top, I climbed atop a huge boulder and sat upon a lush carpet of leaves and ferns. It was a warm sunny day with great fleecy clouds slowly drifting from the west. Across the valley of Diamond Mountain Brook, Eleventh

Mountain rose sharply, its skyline etched with huge virgin spruces.

I remember hearing John Dalaba's voice, clear and bell-like, far down the ridge. As he moved closer, it echoed across the valley. I tried to think of a sound that could be more thrilling.

My contemplation of the splendor of those moments was broken by the rustling of leaves far ahead of me. I took the safe off my rifle. A blue jay screamed. All was quiet again. The rustling gain. Suddenly, far ahead of me, I saw a bear moving my way. Then another one. And heard what I thought to be a third one.

A rifle cracked, then another. Several more shots rang out, filling the valley with echoes. There were shouts, there was wild running toward the action. Then I saw a bear, a very large one, rise on hind legs, rip at a tree. He fell over dead.

John brought a horse and jumper to haul out the bear. There were the stories that night. The next day, we returned to the same place. More shots were fired, two more bears taken, and a third one missed. Again, John brought the horse and jumper. Again, the party of greenhorns were feeling like Daniel Boone as they walked down the trail to camp.

There was, to be sure, a little remorse among us as we looked at the bears prostrate on the autumn leaves, their fur clean and shining black, with short curly hair under the coarse outer fur, their red blood staining the forest floor. But we answered that ancient call, and only one who has heard that call can understand the sensations that such an experience brings.

Teamsters

It is doubtful if any of the great experiences a wilderness hunting party might have had over a period of years exceeds that gratitude they have for the natives who have guided them, toted their tents into favorite campsites, and helped bring the deer or bear out to the clearing.

John Dalaba, whose home and lands adjoined the wilderness, was the first one to help us. In 1925 he guided our first hunting party in the wilderness, and his team of horses hauled out the three bears we managed to get.

Two years later, Johnny Morehouse hauled in our equipment on a wheelless "jumper," a sledlike contraption he made. His son, George, then took us in for several years, but he used a wagon with wheels.

Then for a number of years, the Carl Cleveland family, including his wife and son, Danny, obliged us. He used a jumper at first and then used an old lumber wagon.

For the last eighteen years, Earl Allen, son-in-law of John Dalaba, has taken care of us. His equipment began with conventional wagon wheels and evolved into a wagon with rubber tires.

One year when the teamster's horses died, we built a one-wheel contraption and hauled our equipment by sheer manpower. It was hard work, to say the least, for the trails are rough, often muddy, and there are streams to cross.

Teamsters

Another year, because of similar circumstances, we brought our own horse and had a jumper made for us. It was an exciting and costly adventure we decided not to repeat. These experiences gave us a deep appreciation for the help the mountaineers have furnished.

Man-powered Hauling Rig

Sunshine and Storms
in the Wilderness

Back in hunting camp at Diamond Mountain Brook, our canvas tents are all that shield us from wind, thunder, and snowstorms. At times, winds sweep up the valley from the west so strong that the tent fairly shudders. We tie the tent flaps together and put logs around the base of the tent to minimize the power of the gusts. Occasionally, the crack of a falling tree emphasizes the fury of the storm. In weather too rough for hunting, another log goes in the chunk stove, another pot of coffee is made, and there comes a time for reminiscing—priceless hours for those who love the wilderness.

The sun, rising over the Green Mountains and Lake Champlain thirty-five miles to the east, has to climb an hour or so before its bright shafts reach this part of the wilderness. The crowns of the giant hardwoods are bereft of leaves in late fall, and the sun floods our tent site. From our elevation of 2,000 feet, a long valley to the west and the wild East Branch of the Sacandaga River, with precipitous mountains on each side, provides a fitting backdrop for the sunsets we see from the tent.

Spruce, balsam, and hemlock line the stream course and crown the mountain tops. But the great trunks of virgin yellow birch and maple rule the mountainsides, their limbs often 60 feet above the forest floor.

Numerous streams are born among the high ledges and the evergreens. They drop off cliffs and course through boulder-strewn vales to add tribute to Diamond Mountain Brook in the valley. These gently flowing streams become torrents during and after thunderstorms and snow melts.

One week during the 1960s a series of thunderstorms beset the region. Night after night the thunder echoed between the mountains. Day after day the streams got larger. It was a week of storms. Tiny Deer Brook, which encircles our tents and drops in many little falls around them, became more than 50 feet wide. Every so often, a sound like a rifle shot came from the mountain above us, and another boulder dropped over a falls to the rocks below. That week, Diamond Mountain Brook became so wide and rapid that we would not cross until a giant tree was ripped from its bank and was hurled across the stream, bridging it.

The power of water in these small mountain streams is incredible. Once we found a giant maple hurled to the ground spanning Panther Brook. It had split atwain in the process. And there, resting on the split tree, several feet above the stream bed, was a boulder weighing at least 300 pounds, cast there by the rushing waters of a storm.

On the night of November 8, 1970, we were about to leave home for our wilderness camp when a call came from our forest ranger in North Creek. "Don't come up tonight," he warned. "We already have two feet of snow, and there's a regular blizzard now. Your tent will be flattened." We went in the next day in nearly three feet of snow. The tent was leveled.

We soon had it back up and started to survey our situation. It was still snowing hard. We tried hunting the nearby ridge. It was almost impossible to travel. So we sent one of our party home to pick up snowshoes for everyone.

He was back the next day with the snowshoes. They were useless in the soft snow. The snow and winds continued. The deer were headed toward winter yarding grounds, and we found hunting with any change of success impossible.

Three days later, our teamster came into camp and told us if we wanted to get out before May we had better break camp today. We did. The horses plowed through the snow up to their bellies. They had to literally drag the wagon out; its bed rode atop the snow in the trail.

In the wilderness, weather takes on a strange new dimension. One soon realizes the vast difference between a thin piece of canvas miles back in the woods, and the countless amenities that we are surrounded with by civilization. Our experiences result in a keen appreciation of these opposites.

Trophies

A violent wind-and-rain storm had chased us off Hardwood Ridge to the warm shelter of our tents at the foot of the mountain. It was only ten o'clock in the morning, but we had managed to get thoroughly soaked and chastened by the elements, which were unexpected when we had left camp several hours earlier. Low, heavily laden clouds and fog had settled over the mountains and blotted out the country we all knew so well.

In the warmth and dryness of my sleeping bag, ensconced in fragrant hay, I reminisced. Only a few years ago, I would have persisted and encouraged at least a few of my companions to hunt all day despite the weather. But not anymore. My muscles were tired from five days of hunting, up cliffs, over mountains, and through almost impenetrable swamps. A deer hung on the game pole; the supply tent was well stocked with a variety of favorite vittles. How completely sensible it seemed to spend a day in camp with good friends, good food, and a warm sleeping bag!

The rain pounded on the canvas, and the wind roared and shook the tent frame. The fire crackled merrily in the big chunk stove we had made and lugged in many years ago. I dropped off to sleep.

Before long, I was awakened. It had stopped raining. "Come on, Paul. We're going to hunt the high ledges." I turned over in my bag as if to avoid a bad dream. Some fool is thinking of hunting, I mused. The thought of resting tired muscles all day was a welcome one. Tomorrow would be time enough to take a buck or a bear. Besides, the clouds would be closing in around the top of the mountain that loomed more than a thousand feet above us.

"My woolens are all soaked," I said. "Besides . . . "

"You can take my dry shirt and wear my rain suit," Al said.

It was all over in a few minutes. How could I surrender my youth or at least my youthful spirit so easily? So what if my muscles ached? And if it rained again, I wasn't made of salt, was I?

Soon, five of us stood in front of the tent and planned the hunt, as four, more sensible companions lounged in the complete comfort of camp and had the coffee pot on. As we left, we told them that we would bring back a trophy.

Three of the men headed straight up Deer Brook in back of camp, up along the cataract that tumbles out of a great basin a thousand feet above us. Doc Miller and I headed westerly down the trail along Diamond Mountain Brook past Bear Brook to Panther. Halfway there, we could hear the rumble of its cataract, which now had an abundance of white water cascading over its boulders. We reached the foot of the cataract and started the long climb up the steep mountain slope. It started to rain again.

A ledge, a rest, and the climb again. Smokey clouds scudded through the crowns of virgin maples and yellow birches. The rain came down steadily. Slowly, we climbed toward the high ledges. Occasionally, a blowdown slowed our progress. Breath came short as we labored up precipitous rocks. The air seemed to thin, and a west wind was cold. We began to envy our friends back in the tent.

Soon we were above the great hardwoods and had reached the spruces, tall mastlike trees, 60 feet to the first limbs. Occasionally, we found a moose maple with its bright green bark shredded by the antlers of a buck, ridding the summer velvet that made growth possible. Near the source of the stream, we came to the great spruce that had fallen across a ravine years ago. It was lush now with mosses and fungus and reindeer ferns. It was time for Doc and me to separate and head easterly along cliffs and ledges towards our watchers a mile away on the upper reaches of Deer Brook. I told Doc that I would meet him at High Falls.

A well-worn deer trail came down from the heights to cross this source of Panther. I followed it. Fresh tracks—minutes old—with overturned duff and leaves betraying a large buck. At these high elevations, mosses and ferns grow luxuriantly, watered by the clouds in a chilly atmosphere.

The steepness ended, and I walked out on a relatively flat plateau. It was sprinkled with boulders dropped by glaciers of the Ice Age and studded with several giant spruces centuries old, their black trunks majestic and adding immeasurably to the wildness of the scene. Beyond the plateau, the main mountain rose sharply into the clouds, the fissures in its cliffs garlanded with twisted, dwarf evergreens evolving there for ages.

Near the end of the plateau, a flat tablelike ledge projected from the mountain, and it invited me to tarry. Just as I was about to leave it, the sun broke through the clouds, and patches of blue sky appeared. There was a rustle of wind up along the cliffs, and wisps of clouds were blown into the evergreens to disappear. The sun flooded the mountain with light and shadows that brought into sharp relief rocks and trees.

Looking to the west, I was startled by myriads of raindrops suspended from twigs and needles, sparkling like diamonds, each drop reflecting its wild surroundings.

Far below, Diamond Mountain Brook hurried through the forest to the river. The summits of Bullhead, Puffer, Height-of-Land, and Gore mountains rose in the distance. Encircling them were hills and valleys of the numerous lakes and wetlands.

I felt that I was in the center of a universe of wilderness, filled with beauty and loveliness that reached back into ancient times and would be projected into the indefinite future. Was this what perpetuity means?

If only a great buck would walk into this idyllic setting, a buck with such massive antlers as to grace a page of Boone and Crockett records . . . but no, it was not to be. Just a flight of chickadees flitting from bush to tree and a redheaded woodpecker backing down an ancient dead spruce. From a ledge above me, a red squirrel chattered. All else was still.

I moved from the plateau, still hoping and even half believing that an old buck would bound into reality. A backward glance etched the sparkling raindrops and the splendor of the scene into my memory.

The mountain became steep and brushy. It was a great contrast to the place I had just left. I remembered another similar place and headed for it, to the east along the mountain.

All of a sudden on a ledge just above me, there was a snort, the sound of pointed hoofs hitting rock, the swish of evergreens and . . . silence.

I stood there in petrified motion. The buck had been there. Unquestionably, he had watched me on the plateau. Now he was gone. All that was left was the mountain, the forest, the sunshine, and the blue sky. There were the sparkling raindrops and the mountains beyond.

Far down the mountain, I heard Doc "hounding" it. I answered him with a long, houndlike bay. Soon, I saw him on a lower ledge, and slowly we made our way along the steep slopes, hoping to move a deer or bear toward our watchers along the cataract ahead of us. But there was no rifle shot to echo around the ledges, only sound of the cataract's low rumble broke the stillness. It grew louder and its music more varied as we approached.

Then I caught sight of white water pouring over a ledge dark with evergreens. Just beyond, I heard an expected whistle. Dave Conde's red-clad figure stepped from a hidden glade. "It would have been a great place to see one," he said.

We called up the mountain to Doug Miller. He answered, as did another hunter below. We met at the top of the falls and proceeded down the steep acclivity toward camp. We recalled the many times we had dragged bucks down this very way. Were those moments, so rich with success, more meaningful than these moments?

The cataract plunged downward in a continuous succession of slides, falls, and white water. It chuckled and murmured intermittently, all the while hurrying down to the last falls near our tent. Here and there, icicles clung to shaded ledges. Ferns and mosses bedecked the stream side. At length, we reached a point where we could see the smoke from our tent spiraling upward through the trees. We stopped by a spruce deadfall.

The sun was setting beyond Diamond Mountain Pass, and the sky was laced with streaks of crimson and burnished gold. A first faint star was visible. Immediately below us, white water slid into a pool that reflected the sky. Just beyond it was another, glistening like a silvered mirror. All of us saw the perfection of the scene.

Then, the hunters came out of the tent. "Where's your trophy?" they asked. We smiled. We were loaded with trophies of the wilderness. Those exhilarating hours up among the ledges. The sun breaking through the overcast sky. The myriad of raindrops sparkling in the brilliant light. The thoughts of the great buck bounding up the steep slope. Hours contemplating the splendors of the good earth. From our expressions, they knew they had missed one of the treasured days of a hunt on the high ledges of a wilderness mountain.

Ed Richard and John Hume's Bear
Photograph by Charles Sellers.

An Editor's Bear

We were on the trail to our hunting camp about ten o'clock one November night. It was raining hard as we labored with heavy packs walking single file toward our tents. One of our party was John Hume, an editor of a large newspaper, another was Ed Richard, a guide from the Whitehouse country. Most of us had flashlights.

Suddenly, a large animal came off the nearby ridge and ran between several hunters without lights. We all stopped to look for tracks on the trail. We found them. It had been a bear! "We'll get him tomorrow," I said half seriously. Everybody laughed.

Early the next morning, we were hunting the ridge above camp. By noon, we had two bucks on the game pole. "I never knew there was hunting like this in the wilderness," John remarked. "Oh, we'll get that bear tomorrow," I told him with fingers on both my hands crossed.

The next morning, we hunted the same ridge. I put the watchers in position. I placed John on a creek bank at the foot of a long ridge. I took a position on a high rock some distance from him. The drivers began their hounding, which echoed from the nearby mountain.

Soon, I heard several shots coming from John's stand. When the drive was over, I ran over to where he was. There he stood with a bear on the ground in front of him. As I walked up to him, he extended his hand to me and we shook. With a

John Hume at Camp

John Hume (right foreground) smiles happily as he sits with others around the hunting camp table. That day, he shot the bear that had run between a couple of us as we walked into camp two nights before. Photograph by Charles Sellers.

broad smile he said, "I certainly did not believe you the other night when you said we'd get him!"

I was elated. This was the first time that John had hunted with us. I had invited him because he seemed to be a real sportsman and sincerely interested in what was happening to the Adirondack Mountains. He was helping us immeasurably in our fight to save the deer yarding grounds in the Moose River Plains from being submerged by the proposed Higley Mountain reservoir. His paper published the many news releases we wrote to inform the people of the state about the threat to lands of the New York State Forest Preserve—their lands—by river regulating boards and the power industry.

As he looked down at the bear, he continued, "We'll keep printing those unbelievable stories you are giving us about the Moose River battle."

Snowshoe Rabbit
A snowshoe rabbit on top of Cataract Mountain.

Bear Tracks

The tents at hunting camp had been taken down and hauled to the clearing. It had been a fine season for hunting, but I still did not have enough of it. I enticed the Norwegian twins, Nils and Melvin Engrold, to spend another day on the mountain. "We might see a bear," I told them the night before as we sat beside the cheerful fireplace. Soon the warmth of the fire caused me to doze off.

The morning was crystal clear, about ten degrees above zero, and a fresh snow of several inches had fallen during the night. We headed for the top of Cataract Mountain and crossed the meadow at its foot, then we headed diagonally up the steep slopes toward the summit.

About half way up, we came upon fresh bear tracks headed the same way we were going. We spread apart, agreeing to walk as slowly and quietly as possible. Ten minutes later, I heard Nils shoot. He had seen a bear and missed it. Together, we followed the tracks. It was running uphill as only a bear can run uphill—right through a fallen evergreen tree top, not around it as we had to do.

We reached a point on the mountain just below the summit. The bear had gone into a thick swamp; we followed. The fresh snow showed only the bear's tracks. At the end of the swamp, it had headed straight down the mountain.

We paused and sat on a tree to discuss strategy. Nils and I would follow the bear wherever it went. Melvin would stay nearby in a little clearing where he had a view part way down the steep slopes.

We then took off. The bear plunged straight down the steep slopes, leaping off ledges that we had to go around. At length, we came to the edge of a small cliff where we could look down the mountain for some distance. We saw the tracks enter an opening under a great block of the cliff that had fallen years before. We could hardly believe our eyes. The bear was surely going to be ours. We began wondering how we would drag him back up and over the mountain to the cabin.

Nils agreed to stay atop the cliff and cover me if I ran into trouble. I made my way carefully and cautiously down the mountain to the rock. My nerves were on edge, the safety off my rifle. This was to be the epitome of my hunting experiences. It was like a scenario in a book.

Approaching the entrance where the tracks disappeared, I got within 15 feet of it, scarcely breathing with excitement, when I saw daylight through the crevasse in the rock. The bear had gone through it and headed straight up the mountain in the general direction of Melvin.

Nils joined me, and we started up the steep slopes, hearts pounding, expecting to hear Melvin shoot at any moment. We rested several times and then moved on quickly. We heard a shot. It had to be Melvin. He had to have the bear!

Reaching a point where we were almost in sight of Melvin we heard him shout, "I got one." At the same time we saw where the bear had gone at right angles off the track away from Melvin. We broke through the evergreens and saw Melvin. "I got one," he said. And he held up a white snowshoe rabbit. With a start I awoke. Melvin was shaking my shoulder. "It's time to turn in," he said, "We have to get up and be out early!"

Hunting in a Whiteout

When we left camp that morning, there was a fog that threatened our day's hunt, but hours in the wilderness in November are too precious to waste. We headed for Elm Hill, a mile away and 500 feet higher.

Before we reached this favored place, the fog worsened until you could cut it with your fingers. We found ourselves in the middle of a "whiteout," rare in this part of the Adirondacks.

We gathered together and decided to wait out a change in the weather. As we sat there, we heard a gaggle of geese overhead circling around as though preparing to land on water. They obviously did not know where they were, for there were no lakes or ponds closer than a mile. We agreed that we did not know just where we were either.

When the fog gave no indication of lifting, I suggested that we put on a drive by compass. Irv Taylor was to go southwest for twenty minutes on a brisk walk. He was to leave a man at that point, then turn at right angles, and place men across the land at the usual distance from one another. I was to wait half an hour before beginning a drive with one other man. We checked our compass and began hounding.

Not five minutes later, we heard a single shot. We moved ahead and shortly came to our party. Because it had been so foggy, Irv decided, after placing one man, to forget my instructions. Instead, they found a convenient fallen tree and sat on it. Right after we began the drive, a large buck ran into the center

Large Buck

The fog lifted on our way back to camp after we had taken a large buck. Harry Schrader is standing in the center, Mike DeMarco is kneeling, and I am to the left. Photographer unknown.

of these hunters, turning at the last moment and heading to the left. It came upon the first hunter placed on watch. A single shot ended the hunt.

We all came together, amazed at the success of such an unlikely operation. At that point, we honestly still did not know exactly where we were. We dressed the deer, a fine eight-pointer, and began to consider the best way to go to camp.

Suddenly, the fog lifted and the sun came out.

We quickly found the trail to camp.

Blow Down by the Land Hurricane
Siamese Ponds Wilderness, November 25, 1950.

Hunting in a Hurricane

On November 25, 1950, in the early morning, a hunting companion, Jack Teachout of Galway, and I left my log cabin and headed up Second Pond trail for Elm Hill, which is about four miles to the west. A strong wind at our backs hurried us along. The sky was overcast, and it looked like rain. The gusty wind was cool but not cold. We had gone about two miles along the trail, which winds through a heavy hardwood forest, left it, and climbed Hardwood Ridge to begin our hunt. Giant maples and yellow birches predominate, and here and there a giant spruce or hemlock stand out among lessor beeches. Occasional ledges belied the rocky underlay close to the surface, and giant boulders from the glacial age are sprinkled along the two-mile ridge that points directly to Elm Hill.

As we hunted along, drifting in and out of sight of each other, the day became more eerie. The wind roared louder through Diamond Mountain Pass and along the shoulders of Eleventh Mountain. The sky darkened. Strong gusts pushed us increasingly harder, at times almost blowing us off our feet. We laughed and joked about it. We soon realized that hunting would be impossible when we heard the increasing crashes of heavy limbs being torn from great trees and hurled to the ground.

We came together on Armstrong Hill, decided to head for Elm Hill without delay, have lunch on its rocks, and return to the cabin. By one o'clock, we stood on the ledges where we

83

had taken many a buck over the years. We were looking for a good spot to eat when a huge maple close by started to fall. It tipped crazily, toppling smaller trees with it, and with a loud crash fell into the crotch of another large tree, splitting the second tree atwain. We put our lunches back in our coats and stood there watching the almost unimaginable fury of the wind as it toppled great trees nearby and off in the far distance. When the top 40 feet of a great spruce suddenly cracked and blew almost over our heads, we knew that it was high time to get home.

We headed toward Diamond Mountain trail, believing that in the lower valley we would be safer. We had to lean heavily into the wind to walk at all. The temperature began to fall. Crossing over the ridge, I dropped into a small glen. Three deer jumped out of it, one a large buck. I quickly fired in the darkening woods, and flame spurted from my gun. I missed and was glad I did. Jack came. We unloaded our guns and decided to move as swiftly as possible for the cabin.

Occasionally, a sheet of water came at us horizontally and then inexplicably stopped, leaving us dripping with mist. The moisture dried quickly in the wind. More trees came down, and the sound of breaking timber rumbled across the valley on the mountain. We reached a long spruce ridge that lead to our hunting camp site along Diamond Mountain Brook. As we headed down it, it seemed that the most furious winds of the entire day hit. The tops of big spruces crashed around us. We ran the rest of the way to the brook. There, we saw the wind lifting water from white-water rapids and sending a secondary stream down the valley several feet above the stream itself. Out of breath, we ran to an area of small evergreens, away from large timber, and lay down to recuperate. The noise and the power of the wind were spellbinding.

Rested, we moved as rapidly as we could toward the cabin. More trees came down but none close to us. We reached the cabin, under a darkening sky streaked with yellow.

In the cabin, we built a fire. The wind howled through tiny interstices between the logs, and an occasional gust fairly shook the century-old logs. We talked very little at supper and hit the sleeping bags early.

By the next morning, the wind had stopped. Looking up along the sky line of Eleventh Mountain, once crowned with the spires of giant spruces, we saw only wreckage and great gaps in the once evenly spired silhouette. We learned that nearly half a million acres of trees were blown down in the Adirondack Park, more than half of them on New York State Forest Preserve lands. It was the worst storm in recorded history in the Adirondacks.

The Ruined Vacation

I was at my cabin one Saturday morning in November when I heard wagon wheels banging on rocks coming up the trail and teamsters hee-hawing their animals. A hunter appeared, and I invited him for a cold draft of water at the well. He was a short, middle-aged man, full of enthusiasm, and leader of ten hunters who stopped at the well.

They were going back to the Doug Morehouse camp at The Flow for a two week hunt. (Doug had three guides working for him, and their camp was all set up for such a group.) After introducing himself and his party, the hunter said they had been planning for this trip for a year. "Once we get back there, the rest of the world can go to grass," he said. "We won't be out until it's all over. We'll start hunting on Monday."

It was unseasonably hot for this time of year, and the hunters enjoyed the cold spring water. Two wagons came, heavily loaded. This party, from somewhere downstate, were old hands at this. After they left, I could hear the wagon wheels banging on boulders and the occasional hee-haw of a teamster guiding his horses.

Four days later, I again heard the wagon wheels banging and the teamsters' voices. I was hunting at the foot of the mountain but decided to hurry back to the cabin to see what was going on. I got there just as the leader of the party reached the cabin.

"I thought you were going in for two weeks," I told him. "What happened?"

"They ruined our hunt," he said very much upset. "You'll see when the wagons get here."

The wagons came and stopped by the cabin. I was dumbfounded. There were five antlered bucks and a bear on the first wagon and five bucks on the second.

"Look at that," he said. "Every place the guides put us the deer came through. They completely spoiled our vacation. And it's so hot, the deer will spoil if we don't take care of them right away. They should have had more sense. For a whole year we plan two weeks and all we get is four days!"

With that the men started down the trail, and the wagons followed. I knew the teamster on the second wagon.

He winked at me and grinned.

Bear Hunt

Seven of our hunters had spent the day cutting wood for the coming hunting season. It was early October. After dinner, we gathered in front of the cabin's massive fireplace to discuss plans for the coming hunt. The subject finally came around to bear. We reviewed the years since we had taken one and started discussing how we might triumph again.

The gang suggested all kinds of strategies. None seemed to set any kind of a pattern that might lead to success. The black bear, we agreed, was the most sagacious of the wild creatures we knew. Only rarely does anyone see one, and then the bear quickly disappears in a "rolling ball of rhythm," whether running uphill or downhill.

Outside, the air was frosty and the temperature dropping. We piled logs on the fire and continued to plot out a strategy. When we finally retired to our sleeping bags, we had convinced each other that this fall was the year for a bear.

The following Saturday afternoon, I came again to the cabin. As I neared it, I saw that a back window was out. Inside, the glass had shattered on top of our wood-chunk stove. It looked like someone was looking for something, under cushions, under blankets, in the wood pile. Utensils were scattered on the floor. The cabin was in disarray.

As I started to light a fire in the fireplace, I thought, who would ever do this to me? What did I ever do to deserve what I saw? Something caught me eye. There in the ashes of last week's fire was the impression of the front foot of a large bear. It had raked out the ashes, and its imprint was plainly visible!

The huge section of a Dutch hand-hewn timber we use as a coffee table in front of the fireplace was still in place. The bear must have sat on this beam as he tried to find scraps from the roast we had cooked over the fire. He was not three feet from where three of us sat on a settee the week before, planning his demise! Nor was he more than five feet from the other four men sitting in chairs flanking the settee!

I was so dumbfounded by the audacity of this animal that I went down to our teamster's house and called my fellow guide, Doc Miller, insisting that he come up and see what I saw. An hour later he was there, almost as unbelieving as I.

Several weeks later, our hunters were back in hunting camp. After a long drive, we returned to the tent to find that a bear had ripped a hole in the side and another in the front. He had pulled the tablecloth and all that was on it to the floor. Then, he picked up a bushel of apples from the edge of the bunk and, after carrying them outside, ate all but one. Doc and I looked at each other. We began to wonder who was hunting whom, and who was being most successful!

Early Hunting Camp

Making home in the wilderness. For decades, hunters have looked forward to setting up camp at the beginning of hunting season.

Trackless Snow

It was late November on the edge of winter. I was guiding a party of hunters from Long Island, and we camped in tents at lower Diamond Mountain meadow, four miles back in the wilderness. For three days, the weather had been atrocious—rain, sleet, cold, wind. Now it was snowing hard. We had seen no deer.

Breakfast was over the morning of the fourth day. "Who wants to hunt?" I asked. I opened the tent flaps to look out on a windy snowstorm. "We've had enough," one of the hunters said. "The team is due tomorrow. We'll stay in camp today."

I decided to go alone, hunting the length of Hardwood Ridge to the clearing and then climbing Cataract Mountain to its summit. I would return by following the top of the mountain to a point above the camp. It would be long and difficult.

There were no deer signs of any kind on Hardwood Ridge. The new snowfall, added to 1 foot of old crusted snow, apparently had sent the deer, so plentiful here a few weeks ago, to their winter yarding grounds miles away along the river.

At noon, I headed for the top of Cataract, which was obscured in the snowstorm. I began to question my sanity for even trying to hunt in these conditions. But the crust on the old snow made walking easy through the fluffy snow that had fallen during the past two days.

In about an hour, I reached the relatively level area just below the summit. The storm obliterated the steep northerly slopes. If I were a deer, I mused, I would certainly leave these stormy heights and head for the river in the sheltered lowlands. I found no tracks on the mountain, and I was soon convinced that I should head for the tent and be sensible like the men from Long Island.

The day was largely behind me when I stood on the mountain height that I believed to be directly above the tents in the valley. I knew I must move rapidly to reach camp before dark. A long slide of snow-covered rock was immediately below me. It had no trees or brush on it, and so I sat down and slid about thirty feet to a flat ledge. When I stopped, I found my rifle covered with snow and sat there for a moment while I brushed it off. Just as I was about to stand up, I turned my head. There, standing not 60 feet from me, was an eight-point buck looking right at me. I raised the gun and fired.

I had not seen a deer track all day. Now, I had a magnificent buck and still hadn't seen a track. The deer had been lying down on the ledge in an area protected from the wind by evergreens. It stood only when I had slid down to the ledge.

I reached for my knife to dress the animal and found the sheath empty. I started to drag the 180-pound deer down the steep part of the mountain. When I reached a ravine, I followed the water until I came to a falls where I would let him tumble to its base. There I started dragging him again. Dark was closing in fast, and I was getting exhausted from the extra weight; but I knew if I left the deer the snow might cover it. I kept on dragging until I had reached a more level area I thought was near the tents. I was so tired I decided not to drag it another foot.

Darkness covered the land now, but the snow had stopped. After resting, I finally felt strong enough to move toward camp. To my relief, I found the trail within 15 feet and the tent only a few hundred yards away.

As I looked to the tents with their soft glow coming from the lanterns and the thought of the men comfortable inside, I decided to be nonchalant, even though I had never felt so successful. I opened the flap and looked at my party of thoroughly discouraged hunters.

"Did you see any?" I was asked.

"Yes, a very nice one."

"With antlers?"

"Great ones."

"Get a shot?"

"Yes, one. How about a cup of coffee?"

"Did you hit him?"

"Yes."

"How do you know?"

"As soon as I finish this coffee, we'll go down the trail and drag him back here," I said. They didn't know whether to believe me or not, but they all started to follow me with their flashlights after I downed the coffee and headed back outside.

When we reached the buck, there by the side of the trail, they went almost crazy. They jumped up and down and slapped me and each other on the back. We gutted it, and they dragged it up to the tents. That initial exuberance was nothing like the reaction I got when I told them that all I wanted of that deer was a hind quarter . . . that they could have the rest and take it to Long Island and brag about how they got it!

Coyote

Eight inches of new snow covered the wilderness. Deer seldom move about immediately after such a storm. It was bitter cold. I decided to walk down the trail along Diamond Mountain Brook to a spruce-and-hemlock grove about a mile away. Halfway down, I struck the tracks of a good sized coyote. They stopped suddenly about a hundred yards away; the animal lunged to the left, hitting something buried in the fresh snow. There was nothing visible but a few feathers and a few drops of blood. A ruffed grouse had taken refuge for warmth in the light fluffy snow. In some mysterious way the coyote sensed it was there.

The Lost Tent

Problems at one of my construction jobs had held me up from meeting my friends at the cabin for the Friday-night hike into the hunting camp. It was nine o'clock when I reached Baker's Mills. Snow was falling with large flakes that limited visibility to 30 feet. I figured I might just as well take my time getting back into camp. Everyone would be sleeping by the time I reached the tents. I stopped at a favorite diner and had conversation with a forest ranger.

It was still snowing when I was ready to leave, and the ranger suggested I not make the trip until morning. "Its a bad night to travel the woods," he admonished me. But I assured him I could find my way back there blindfolded if necessary.

I drove to my cabin several miles away, adjusted my pack heavy with some goodies for camp, and started in. As I started up the trail, I had to admit that I had never seen a snowstorm as heavy as this one. Five inches of snow had already fallen atop a crust from earlier storms. After I had walked about half a mile, I also had to concede that the landmarks, so indelibly impressed in my mind as a result of numberless trips this way, were not recognizable. Several times, I walked off the trail and into the adjacent woods because everything looked alike. I found myself breaking through the crust whenever I got off the trail.

Suddenly, I realized I was no longer on the trail. I decided to head straight up a gentle grade until I reached Height-of-Land, from which point it would be a gentle grade downward to camp. If necessary, I would follow the creek that flowed nearby.

I finally reached the crest of the trail. I moved to my right, downhill, expecting to find Diamond Mountain Brook. I found myself walking uphill again. The stream was not where I thought it ought to be. I began to tire from breaking through the old crust without snowshoes. Perhaps someone would hear me if I gave a hounding call. I climbed on a huge boulder I had not remembered seeing before and gave some long houndlike bays. The snow-filled atmosphere swallowed up the calls. Strangely, I heard no echo from Cataract Mountain.

The wet snow kept covering my glasses, so I took them off. My flashlight batteries were getting noticeably weaker. It was then that I began to realize that back in the tent were fresh batteries, my compass, waterproof matches, rifle, and sleeping bags.

After a good rest, I started to move to what appeared to be downhill toward the hunting camp. I thought I recognized some of the huge maples and yellow birches that are sprinkled throughout our hunting territory. They stood majestically in the heavy storm.

As I walked toward the tents, the thought of them never before seemed so homelike. Never before had I so ardently wished that I was there with my friends. I called again. The silence was deafening. I started to move as rapidly as possible.

Soon, I sensed a gentle, steady downgrade. I kept breaking through the crust. Each step became more difficult. The storm seemed to let up. Through the snowflakes I saw a light. It disappeared. I saw it again. I knew where I was. The boys had hung out a lantern for me.

Once again, the light shined clearly. The storm was abating. I knew exactly where I was. I moved in the direction of the light. I was extremely pleased with myself for getting out of such nonsense. Of course, I would never tell my friends I had been mixed up. After all, I was their guide!

The truth came as a shock. The light was not at our tent.

The light was a highway light at Baker's Mills two miles down the valley!

Some guide, I thought, as I headed into the now familiar woods near my cabin. Reaching there, I threw my pack on the floor, found an old sleeping bag, and exhausted, quickly fell asleep. Of course I could never tell my friends anything about this!

Hugh Lackey and a Kitten

Hugh Lackey holds a kitten that followed him three miles into the wilderness. Nils and Melvin Engvold stand on either side of him. Our guide, George Morehouse, is at the right.

Game Warden

We were back in camp for our annual hunt. A fine buck was hanging from the game pole. Our guide, George Morehouse, had gone out to the clearing the day before and was due back this morning. Because we had changed our plans and decided to hunt Bog Meadow country, we had to get word to him to save three extra miles of walking. In camp with us were Melvin and Nils, identical Norwegian twins. Melvin agreed to go out to the clearing and tell George where to meet us. He headed out at a dog trot.

Melvin had gone about half a mile along the trail when he saw Mark Stewart, the game warden, coming towards him. Melvin recognized him by his hat. For reasons he never could explain, as soon as he saw that hat, he jumped off the trail and hid behind a large maple. The warden stopped and asked Melvin what the trouble was. Embarrassed, Melvin came to the trail and said that nothing was the matter. He proceeded at a dog trot toward the clearing.

After checking several deer runs on the way, the warden reached our tents just as we were finishing breakfast. We invited him in and offered him a cup of hot coffee. He sat down at the table directly opposite Nils. The warden looked at him and then looked at me and then at Nils again. He took a sip and started chatting about our hunt and the number of deer we were seeing. We went about our business of readying for the day's hunt. As we were about to leave, the warden told us that he wanted to check out a few things before he left.

We met George and went on to Bog Meadow. During the course of the day, Melvin told us about meeting the warden and how stupid he felt about hiding behind the tree. It was then I realized why the game warden kept looking at Nils and me, as though questioning something about us. When we returned to camp that afternoon, the warden was gone.

Early the next year, I was walking down the main street in North Creek and ran into Mark Stewart. He stopped, and we talked a bit. Then he said, "Paul, you've got to clear this up for me. Why in tarnation did one of your hunters try to hide from me? And how did he get back to camp so quickly? He wasn't even breathing hard when I had coffee with you that morning."

I laughed. "The man you saw in the tent was an identical twin to the one you saw on the trail," I replied. The expression on Mark's face was priceless. "Well I'll be," he grumbled. "You know I spent half of that day near your camp looking for an illegal deer!"

His Last Hunt

Guy Jones was president of the Schenectady County Conservation Council and a very distinguished conservationist.
After one of the meetings, a group of us were talking about
deer hunting and our pursuit of this wonderfully sagacious
denizen of the North Woods.

I've tried for forty years to get a set of antlers," Guy told
us. "I've been in the most deer-abundant sections of the
Adirondacks with some of the best guides. In all that time, I've
never even seen a legal buck. It's time for me to give up. Besides
I'm seventy years old."

His statement intrigued us. We decided to arrange one
more hunt for this dedicated sportsman. Several weeks later, I
talked to my friend Ed Richard, one of the best known guides
of the Silver Lake Wilderness. He agreed to join my party and
Guy Jones in a weekend hunt. Before long, nine of us were
back at our hunting camp in the wilderness.

Early on the first morning, we stood in the meadow at the
base of the falls of a brook that is born near the top of the
mountain. We had decided that our first hunt would be the
precipitous lower western summit of Cataract Mountain. We
asked seven of the party to place themselves up along the brook
on one side of its ravine. Ed and I would go around the base of
the mountain, climb it, and start the drive down to where the
men were in the valley. As the watchers started up the brook,
Ed and I decided that one of them should be here at the foot of
the mountain. I called up, and Guy came down.

101

A Cook in Hunting Camp

Although our hunting party always had several men who enjoyed cooking for the group, in the 1950s we decided to add an hour or more each day to our hunting time by hiring a cook. On our third attempt, we hired a man with some credentials—he had once owned a string of restaurants in New York and turned our limited fare, including venison, into gourmet meals. He livened his meals with wonderful stories of how he bought a silver mine in the Mexican wilderness and had several hundred Mexicans working for him. The day he finished an expensive railroad line to the mine, the Mexican government appropriated it and left him ruined.

"We want you to watch here," we told him. He laughed. "I had decided not to go any further up the mountain," he said, "I guess the boys forgot how old I am."

The three of us walked about a hundred feet along the base of the mountain. I pointed up to the steep slope where we could see a depression in the ridge about 75 yards away. "The deer will come down through that notch," I assured him. He laughed heartily. "They've been telling me that for forty years," he replied.

Ed and I took off, walked along the mountain for a while, and then headed straight up its steep slopes. We reached the summit, quite out of breath, and started back down. Every so often, we would come to a cliff we had to go around or stand on a ledge. I began to think that this was quite ridiculous, but there were deer tracks on every ledge.

When we were about half way down, we heard a shot come from far below. Then a second. "That's Guy Jones," Ed remarked. We hastened around a ledge and down the steep hard-

---

On our first day in camp, the cook told us that out in those mountains was a great buck that we were to get without delay. We brought into camp a fine large-antlered buck. He dismissed it as not being what he had asked for. Everyday that week, we brought in another buck, expecting a compliment. Everyday, we were disappointed. On Saturday night, he reminded us at dinner that we had not gotten the deer he said was out there waiting for us.

The next morning, we were up early. The teamster was due at noon. By 10:30 A.M., everything was packed and ready to go. One of the men suggested that we had time for a short hunt up behind the camp. The cook urged us to get "the one" out there waiting for us.

By noon, we were back. The cook heard us coming and met us at the edge of the woods. He clapped his hands. "That's the one I've been telling you boys about!," he shouted. He got a camera and took this picture. Today, people who come to the Adirondack Room in my home can see the results of the cook's challenge.

wood forest toward Guy. We saw him. He waved. As we drew closer we saw him standing behind a fine eight point buck!

"Three came down right where you said they would!" his voice resonated with excitement. "I could have had another!" He told this to each of the watchers as they reached us. "I just can't believe what happened. It's worth a lifetime of waiting!"

Guy did his share to drag the deer out, split wood at the tent, and busied himself making supper. It was plain to see that Guy had regained his youth.

For five successive years, Guy joined us in camp each fall, hunted with us, and each year took a fine antlered buck! When he finally stopped hunting at age seventy-five, we found that he had taken five bucks with six shots.

None of us have bettered his record.

Winter Deer Feeding Experiment

Anyone who hunts white-tailed deer for a long time becomes concerned with their general welfare. In the Adirondacks, weather is a more severe factor for the deer herd than elsewhere in the state. Snows usually come a week or two earlier, and frigid conditions last several weeks longer in the spring. The period when deer can range freely is from two to four weeks shorter than in other parts of the state. As soon as substantial snowfall occurs, the deer move from hardwood ridges and mountain tops where food is plentiful to sheltered coniferous valleys along rivers and streams where food is less abundant. In such valleys, beaver ponds are often found, and there numerous plants beneficial to deer grow. In the valleys, deer are protected from sub-zero winds and have access to the essential running water. As snows deepen, the deer make narrow trails. They can move freely and have some protection from predators, but food is limited.

The winter of 1930 was very severe, and it took its toll on the herd. Hundreds of deer died of starvation. It occurred to me that the deer might be helped if hay, found in a place such as Second Pond Flow (which was part of a deeryard), was cut in late summer and stacked for them to eat. I wrote to the New York State Conservation Department suggesting it.

The Conservation Department agreed to pay mountaineers to cut tons of hay on the large meadow of state land near Second Pond. The hay was stacked and fenced. When the heavy

Stacked Hay for Deer
Hay stacked for winter deer feeding experiment at Second Pond Flow.

snows came, the hay was distrbuted to various locations easily
accessible for the deer. This experiment was carried out for a
number of years until it was finally concluded that such winter
feeding of deer had long-term negative results.
The idea was abandoned.

Wilderness Deer

This is the only photograph of a living deer in the wild that I was able to take in over sixty years of wilderness hunting. The elusive wild deer are very different from the tamed deer that come to feeding stations or are kept in captivity.

Adirondack Wilderness

Siamese Ponds Wilderness

The Siamese Ponds Wilderness consists of nearly two hundred square miles of land in the New York State Forest Preserve. This beautiful, pristine area is classified as "wilderness" and is adjacent to Cabin Country. Photograph by New York State Department of Environmental Conservation.

Cabin Country adjoins the 200-square-mile Siamese Ponds Wilderness, which is part of the New York State Forest Preserve* in the Adirondack Park. The park consists of about 6 million acres of land in both public and private ownership. About half of these lands are owned by the people of New York State and are protected by the famous "forever wild" covenant in the New York State Constitution:

> The land of the state, now owned or hereafter acquired, constituting the forest preserve as now fixed by law, shall be forever kept as wild forest lands. They shall not be leased, sold, or exchanged, or taken by any corporation, public or private, nor shall the timber be sold, removed, or destroyed.

The Siamese Ponds Wilderness is one of sixteen areas set aside in the Adirondack Forest Preserve where the use of motorized vehicles, including aircraft, is prohibited. The region has fifty-one mountains, sixty-seven lakes, and miles of rivers and streams. It is a land of deer, bear, fisher, otter, bay lynx, and other innumerable wood folk. It is a land of silence and solitude set aside to transcend time and man.

The area is bordered by Thirteenth Lake on the north, the

---

*Editor's Note: *Defending the Wilderness: The Adirondack Writings of Paul Schaefer* (Syracuse University Press, 1989) chronicles more than half a century of conservation work in New York State and shows Schaefer's visionary role as one of the state's greatest conservationists. During this period, the American value placed on "wilderness" changed from one that sought destruction to one of reverence for nature's intrinsic values. Schaefer's efforts to attain harmony between man and nature have helped to secure an irreplaceable heritage for generations yet to come.

Adirondack Rocks

The glaciers that carved the Adirondacks about 12,000 years ago left evidence of their power that is difficult to comprehend. The entire park is littered with sections of cliffs ripped from high mountains and cast aside hundreds of miles from the place of origin. Most imposing is this glacial erratic that lies in an overgrown field near the cabin. It is almost round, stands about 30 feet high, and is slightly longer. Its shape was sculpted by the glacial action that ground it against such hard rocks as anorthosite and the solidified molten rock that makes up the Adirondacks.

East Branch of the Sacandaga River on the east, the Middle Branch of the Sacandaga on the south, and Indian Lake on the west.

Trails from many directions penetrate into the wilderness region. The trail that passes my cabin door, known as the Second Pond Flow trail, has two main branches deep in the woods. One is the Diamond Mountain Brook trail which leads to our hunting camp, and the other is the ancient trail to Second Pond and nearby mountain country. Beyond the East Branch of the Sacandaga River, which bisects the region, there are more than 20,000 acres with no trails except those of wood folk. It is a place where one can enter with a full burden of the cares of civilization on one's back and quite suddenly find that the burdens have lifted and that a strange, new song fills one's heart. This is emphasized when standing on a high cliff brink where no evidence of man is visible in the sea of mountains that roll on to far horizons. In this country, one feels a kinship with all nature and finds peace and tranquility, the grail he or she has been seeking.

Skyledge Cataract

A thick sphagnum swamp on the high east shoulder of Cataract Mountain feeds this stream. In freshet time, the stream can be 50 feet wide, dropping 1,000 feet.

Cataract Mountain

More than two centuries ago, surveyors running a line of one of the great pre-Revolutionary land grants, established a corner, one of thousands, on a wild and beautiful mountain in Warren County. It marked a corner of the Eleventh Township of the Totten and Crossfield Purchase of more than 1 million acres. Thus by an accident of exploration a mundane name was given to a mountain rich with unique natural features. On maps it is called Eleventh Mountain.

Half a century ago, a number of us who hunted that mountain and were enthralled by its magnificence, decided to give it a more fitting name. "Cataract Mountain" it has been and is for us, U.S. Geological Survey maps notwithstanding. Five crystal streams tumble off the thickly forested peak that stretches 3,249 feet in elevation. Some of the cataracts that form are spectacular.

On an eastern plateau, there is a great sphagnum swamp which receives drainage from the nearby summit. Its stream, fed by rain, snow, and clouds, drops over a ledge; and in a series of slides and falls and boulder-filled pools, it drops more than 1,000 feet to the valley below. In freshet time, the stream sometimes reaches a width of 50 feet and is visible from Route 8, 2 miles south of Baker's Mills. At one such time, Sigurd Olsen, well-known conservationist and writer from Minnesota, stood with other members of the Wilderness Society on the road looking at it. "I have never seen anything like it," he said.

Pothole

This pothole sits high on a side ledge of the East Branch of the Sacandaga River, well above the current stream bed. The stones in it ground out the bedrock of the river. It is hard to envision the quantity of water that one time flowed down the river from unknown watersheds.

"All that water coming from just a high mountain swamp. It's incredible."

This stream is the ultimate source of North Creek, from which the Adirondack hamlet got its name. The stream meets the Hudson River about 10 miles northeast of the mountain.

Four other streams also rise near the summit and drop off the north side of the mountain into Diamond Mountain Brook, which is tributary to the East Branch of the Sacandaga River. In the Adirondack Park, the rivers—like the land—are classified into wild, scenic, and recreational rivers according to their character and use. The East Branch of the Sacandaga River is in the wild classification of the Adirondack rivers system. Deer, Bear, Panther, and Cataract brooks are all within half a mile of each other. Deer Brook encircles our hunting camp and is close to Diamond Mountain Brook, which heads directly to the river.

This north side of the mountain is heavily forested with virgin hardwoods and clumps of spruce near the top. Before the great land hurricane of 1950, the long ridge just below the summit was parklike; relatively level for a mile and a half, with great cliffs buttressing it, it had little brush of any kind but was rich with ferns and mosses. An occasional deer trail crosses it and disappears either in the great swamp near the top or down the steep mountainside to the open hardwood country. In all the years I climbed and hunted that mountain, I never saw anyone other than the members of our hunting party there.

There are numerous spots where I can stand on a rocky ledge above the precipitous forested slopes dropping off to the valley far below and experience a solitude so wonderful that it causes emotions I cannot describe. At such times, my mind wanders to Mt. Alvernia in Italy, where Francis of Assisi had his hermitage and where his friars have been guarding the trees and plants there for more than 700 years. Here on Cataract Mountain—protected by the "forever wild" covenant—the work of the Divine Artist is all about us, from the lichens clinging to the bare rocks to the hawk wheeling in the sky far above.

East Branch of the Sacandaga River
with Cataract Mountain in the background

The mountain's profusion of gorges, ledges, acclivities, and thickets give deer and bear an almost perfect habitat that is quite free from the dangers of man. Once they reach the swamp just below the main summit they are safe.

I could write a book about our experiences on that mountain. It would be one, for the most part, that would tell how the natural conditions of the mountain prevented us from achieving our much-labored hunting goals—that is precisely what makes Cataract Mountain so wonderful!

Beaver

If it were not for the activities of beaver, both in ancient times and today, the Siamese Ponds Wilderness would be an almost unbroken forest, except for lakes and wetlands. Scattered throughout the region are meadows, both large and small where from time immemorial these busy engineers have built their dams, flooding out heavy forest and leaving a permanent impression upon the country.

Every year we see evidences of this fact. What was a lovely spruce, balsam, and tamarack swamp in the heart of our country for decades is a series of beaver ponds. Water exits from both ends of this half-mile lowland between Gilbert Hill and Blackcat Mountain. For many years, a favorite drive there almost always produced shots at deer. There also was a bear wallow near an edge of the swamp, and often bears would be startled by our drives. Deep game trails wound among the scattered softwoods, and many unusual plants and flowers grew there. At the most westerly end of the swamp, there was a natural clearing about 100 feet in diameter just below some cliffs. Deep sphagnum mosses and bordering tamaracks made this pool a gem of the botanical world. It is now flooded.

But a land scattered with beaver ponds vastly improves deer hunting. The open areas created by the ponds are favorite places for deer because they feed from the many plants and shrubs that surround their edges. Deer trails coming off the mountains and ridges lead directly to these sunny oases in the

The Bridge

Beaver dams serve as bridges across ponds and wetlands. They are used by all kinds of animals, including birds and man. Most are hazardous crossing for man. Beaver dams vary from 5 to 15 feet in width at the base, rising to a narrow, slippery mass of limbs and mud at the top. Many a person has wished that he or she had taken the long way around the pond after having slipped and fallen into icy water and having gotten soaked on a cold or snowy day.

deep woods. Such lands, reverting to the way they were more than a century ago, are also ideal habitat for moose. Moose from Canada and Maine are returning to these ancient lands.

Beaver Pond Trout

A few years ago we were following a deer trail along a remote Adirondack stream in the land that lies "back o'yonder." We had reached a region as near to being wilderness as may yet be found in our eastern America. The trees were ancient and patriarchal, and despite a hot August sun, they kept the forest cool and green. They maintained the stream that alternately idled in darkened pools and hurried over rock and riffle into the forest preserve.

At length, there was an abrupt falling away of the upland valley where the stream wound. We came upon a cataract that tumbled one hundred feet in successive stages into a valley below. Reaching it, we discovered a mountain basin of striking beauty. An old mountaineer had told me about this "green valley." The evergreens marched in unbroken ranks from the open meadow of the flats to the surrounding mountain ridges; the brook meandered snakelike through the basin nearly one-quarter of a mile long. Except for a scattering of alders and popple, the valley was open and indicated the presence at one time of a beaver colony. Here, surely, would be trout!

In a few minutes, we had a rod together and were casting carefully in inviting pools. An hour later, we had reached the conclusion that there were trout here, but they seldom exceeded the minimum legal size. We wondered why.

Four years later, lacking a few months, we again walked down the identical deer path along the stream that of old had

Beaver Pond

Nature indeed had been at work in the four years between our visits and transformed a relatively barren mountain valley into a fisherman's dream.

so taken our interest. The cataract was the same except that the water was higher, the pools deeper, and the melody of wild water was stronger.

Just below, I told my pack-laden friend, was the "green valley," where one's mind snapped a photograph which flashed in one's memory innumerable times during the hustle of city life. We would camp close by the stream where a peninsula of balsams reached down to the water from the hills.

We dropped over the last ledge to the meadow, but the meadow had disappeared. Instead, a quarter of a mile of water, shimmering in the sunlight, greeted our eyes. A new beaver dam!

We hadn't reached the shoreline before a flock of ducks with a loud whirring of wings took off from the water. A beaver house was near the shore. There was a chorus of red-winged blackbirds and an unforgettable medley of hordes of tree frogs and peepers along the water's edge. Suddenly, a trout broke water not 30 feet away!

We quickly assembled our rods and began working the still, dark waters. An hour later, we sat on a balsam point not far from the beaver dam. In our creels was the legal limit of native brook trout, thick and orange and beautiful.

As the sun went down and the campfire lit the surrounding forest with its cheerful light, I could not help but reflect upon the magic wrought upon that valley by the beavers. Not 6 feet high nor more than 100 feet long, the beaver's natural dam had transformed a relatively barren mountain valley into a fisherman's dream by giving the existing trout more water, more space, and more food.

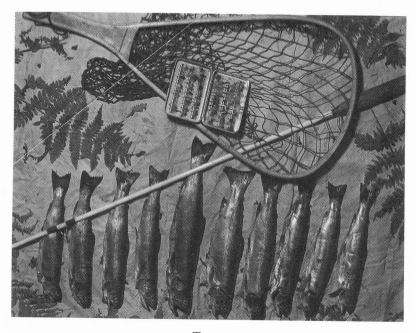

Trout

Adirondack streams are abundant with trout in early spring, after the ice goes out of the lakes and most of the snow melts off the mountain. Photograph by Ellis Edgar.

Early Trout Fishing

In the crew of carpenters and other craftsmen who worked for me, there were a number of avid fishermen. During lunchtime, I often told them stories of fishing and the considerable success I had experienced in the north country. My foreman, Irv Taylor, and carpenter, Al Cowin, were eager for me to take them trout fishing to my favorite wilderness waters early in the springtime before the rush of other fishermen got the best ones. I told them I never met any fishermen back in my country. They didn't believe me.

One winter they urged me to take them right after the season opened in April. I told them it was too early, that fishing would not be good in the wilderness until May 15. Both of them, I think, believed I was saving the early days of the season for myself. When they pressed me to go in April, I told them the snow would still be in the woods, and the lakes would still be frozen over. By then in Schenectady, the snow was already gone and the Mohawk River was free of ice. So, they assumed winter would be gone up north, too. Without telling me, they decided to go anyway.

It was a weekend in late April. When they reached the cabin, they found no snow in the fields, although there was some visible on the mountain. Shouldering their heavy packs, they headed up the Flow trail. Once they reached Height-of-Land, nearly 2,300 feet in elevation, the snow was more than a foot deep and crusty. They began to have doubts about the wisdom

125

of the trip but finally decided that the lake would be free of ice. (I had told them that as soon as the ice went out trout fishing would be at its best.) They began to feel the weight of their packs. When they had gone about 2 miles on the trail, they came to the junction where Second Pond trail leads off to the right. They decided that is where they would go.

The trail had not been cleared for several years, and they soon found themselves off of it. Al began to overheat and took off his new expensive plaid coat. He hung it in a tree, expecting to get it on the way out. By then, it was pitch dark in the woods. They continued ahead with flashlights. They soon realized that they did not really know where they were, but believed if they kept going north they would reach Second Pond.

They were exhaused because they kept breaking through the crust of the snow. Almost ready to give up, Irv saw ahead of him a lake. The men figured they had made it. Reaching the lakeshore they made camp, built a fire, and hit the sleeping bags. They were too exhausted to get much sleep.

When dawn came, they looked out on a small lake. There was no snow on its surface. It was still quite dark. Al quickly got his pole together and attached his bait to the hook. He made care not to entangle his line in the trees and cast his bait as far as possible. It slid across the lake's surface of ice! Thoroughly disillusioned, they got their packs together and started for home. On the way out, they decided to try a shortcut and forgot about Al's new coat hanging on a tree.

It was quite a while before either of them told me about their fishing trip. And when they did, I was able to add a bit of irony to their story.

The lake they reached was Mud Pond. It is the only lake I know of in the Siamese Ponds Wilderness that, for some reason or other, does not have any fish of any kind in it!

Elk

Members of my hunting parties often included men from many parts of the world who lived in the Schenectady region and worked at the General Electric Company. One such individual was an engineer from Colorado, who had hunted extensively in the west.

One November afternoon, we were walking on the homeward trail to camp and heard a strange sound from the top of the mountain. Our friend stood transfixed at the sound. "That," he said, "is an elk bugling." We laughed, but he came right back. "I've hunted elk all over the west, and that was an elk. No question." On the following day, we hunted near the top of that mountain. In a draw where a stream began, we found tracks twice as large as deer. We began to believe our friend.

A year later on October 30, 1946, a reporter for the *New York Daily Mirror*, who was hunting at the North Woods Club, located about twenty miles north of our mountain. He killed a 520-pound elk with massive antlers.

The last elk introduced in the Adirondacks was by the Litchfield family up near Tupper Lake about 1920. How such a large animal and the others necessary for his existence could have survived that long without being seen is a mystery we probably will never solve.

Cliff Flower

Diamond Mountain Brook flows westerly into the East Branch of the Sacandaga River through a lovely valley between Cataract and Diamond mountains in the Siamese Ponds Wilderness. The valley narrows, and the mountains rise precipitously on both sides of the brook. On the north is a shoulder of Diamond Mountain. From the brook to the base of 100-foot cliffs that form the crest of this mountain is a forest of virgin hardwoods, notable giant maples, and yellow birch, many with first limbs 60 feet above the ground.

One day in late November, I climbed the mountain, which alternates in steeps and terraces with an occasional small brook dropping in miniature falls and leafy pools frequented by wildlife. On the top of the cliffs, there were abundant fresh deer signs, and numerous trees barked by the bucks ridding their horns of summer velvet. A fresh track dropped off the cliffs through a natural cut in the rocks, and I followed it down to where it turned and went horizontally along the talus slope. It then veered sharply upward about 25 feet and crossed a little grotto-like niche in the ancient cliffs. A flat ledge invited me to rest and have lunch. The warm sun of high noon flooded the niche. A great block of stone had fallen where it would block the normally steady west winds that sweep along the valley. Today, all was still.

Across the valley half a mile away was the spruce-clad rampart of Cataract Mountain, rising precipitously from about the 2,500-foot level. I tried to locate in the mass of green clinging to the cliffs a tiny cave in that great rampart I had found or dreamed of years before. I could hear the music of the stream far below me and the muted roar of a cataract just visible on the mountain's lower levels. A small spruce had fallen close to where I sat, and I gathered a handful of dried branches, contemplating a tiny fire to toast my lunch.

Something caught my eye. Near the center of this little grotto, amid scattered scarlet and gold leaves, lifting a snow white blossom above its green mantle, was a white violet of unusual size. Just one. A violet in November? The harbinger of early springtime, usually growing along lowland trails, here amid rocks with almost no soil except in its tiny locale and right on the edge of winter. I knelt to catch its faint fragrance and tossed away the twigs for the fire. I marveled, as I do so often, at the infinite variety and wonders of nature.

Mud in Bog Meadow Swamp

One summer's day after about a week of hot, humid weather, I came upon a dried-up pool of mud near the center of Bog Meadow Swamp. It looked like thin ice upon which an object had been dropped. How could mud be of such consistency as to cause such an infinity of cracks? What fell to make the cracks?

Ice Balls on the Mountain

Late one November afternoon, I was making my way toward hunting camp from the high ledges of the mountain. Having walked briskly for some time, I found myself thirsty and came upon a small brook coursing down through the open hardwoods in a shallow ravine. I walked down it a little way until I came to where the stream dropped over a short ledge and splashed onto a large, flat boulder.

Stooping down to get a drink, I saw scores of nearly-perfect round ice balls, one-half-inch to three-quarters inch in diameter. They were on low bushes and on the overhang of the boulder. A few joined together like a necklace. The last faint rays of the sun caused some to sparkle.

After quenching my thirst, I collected a pocket full of them and hastened to camp. There I found my companions about ready to have a nip of Southern Comfort. I laid a few on the table, put the rest in a pail, and rinsed them in the nearby brook. My hunters thought I was pulling some kind of a joke.

It wasn't until I offered to take them to the brook that they finally believed me.

Nate Davis Pond

In 1960, Ed Zahniser and I looked out from my cabin at some small mountains south of Crane Mountain and decided to find out what might lie between them. When we were almost turned back in our exploration by a thick swamp, we came upon a glacial lake that was not depicted on county, state, or federal maps. I took some photographs of it to the chief of land acquisition of the New York State Conservation Department. the state's records showed no waters of any kind in the bowl of these mountains. The current maps show the lake with topographic lines passing through it.

Edward's Hill Road

Johnny and Carolyn

E dward's Hill Road climbs two miles into the highlands from Route 8. When I turn off the highway, I enter Cabin Country. The drive along the road brings back years of memories, not just of the mountains, forests, rivers, and lakes but of the wonderful people who live there. Many of them are descendants of the original settlers who forged worthy lives from the beauty and harshness of the mountains. Many others, like myself, come for renewal. Some come and stay, others come when possible.

Many of the older folks I have written about have died, but their personalities are cherished. Especially vivid are memories of some of our first days here when mountaineers played their fiddles and held square dances in the house where we lived. Never before had I heard "Turkey in the Straw" and the many other mountain songs. Other members of our family enjoyed people whom I never really got to know. They were extraordinarily generous to my mother and younger sister when they stayed in the mountains and we went back to work in the cities. They often gave us milk, eggs, butter, maple syrup, berries, trout, and venison that kept our family going.

There are many questions I forgot to ask these mountain people years ago. Did the first settlers on Edward's Hill come from New England? Did they cross Lake Champlain by boat or over the ice? How rich was their bounty from the wilderness? Who built the old log cabin? When? Who settled west of the Dalaba farm where there is now but an indentation in the Siamese Ponds Wilderness to mark the cabin site? Did his children attend school in the old log school house, now returned to the soil, that stood near the Dalaba Spring Brook? What about "Bob Cat" Ranney and "Uncle Billy"? And the shot one midnight in 1929, followed by a fire that leveled a barn? Edward's Hill is rich in history that I don't know.

Perhaps, some of the answers to these questions are known by the children, grandchildren, and great-grandchildren of my friends, who are still part of the mountains. Without an agricultural base, they depend on other occupations, such as mining, logging, highway maintenance, maple sugaring, banking, and law enforcement. John Dalaba's daughter, Daisy Allen, is a minister, and her husband, Earl guides hunting parties into the wilderness and each spring taps his sugar bush to produce fine maple syrup. Most of these people are excellent hunters and fishermen. They are the true Adirondackers.

My brothers and sisters all come to the mountains. Each of us has our own cabin either on Edward's Hill or on roads nearby, and most of the cabins look to Crane Mountain. We have found our own expressions to preserve the mountains and have passed on to our children and grandchildren the wilderness values that have been so critical in the shaping of our lives.

In the summer, we gather at a Schaefer family reunion. Now nearly seventy people come to celebrate. Invited are some close friends, such as the Zahnisers, who have shared generations of experiences. Others come from many different states, each bringing a different perspective, each bound by a love for the mountains.

As I drive up the road that changes to dirt, I see what the years have yielded. The camp my father bought, the old log cabin, and Beaver House, a cabin I built in the 1950s. These places have played a significant role in my life and bring back treasured memories of people and events that make up Cabin Country. Soon, I will turn into the path that takes me to Beaver House, and I know another adventure will start.

Carolyn and the Kids

The Mohawk Valley Hiking Club was a blessing for a score of kindred souls who enjoyed the long brown paths and the great out of doors. Week after week, the group, of which Carolyn and I were members, explored the Mohawk, Hudson, and Schoharie river valleys, the surrounding hills, and mountains. We walked along the rivers, up the streams, over hill and dale, and explored bottomless caves. We visited deserted houses, looked for Indian relics, and became aware of wildlife, plants, and flowers. We also made friends with farmers, men and women of the hill country, and even with an Indian who promised to lead us to an unknown chamber in a great cave. Soon the trips found us on Dome Island on Lake George, atop Black, Cat, and Tomany mountains, at North Creek, and even at the 1932 Winter Olympics at Lake Placid. Usually, there were about twenty men and women of all ages that went on the outings.

Carolyn was an extremely popular member of the group. Her home on a farm on the Normanskill gave her a background that brought a new and interesting element into the lives of those of us who were city-oriented.

After our marriage in 1935, we went north to the old log cabin at every opportunity. We climbed the nearby mountains and explored the wilderness. There, our four children, Mary, Evelyn, Francis ("Cub"), and Monica spent their summers with Carolyn, hiking and camping. Often, they were joined by the growing family of Howard Zahniser. The Zahnisers' cabin was

137

The Four Schaefer Children

Aspiring 46'ers on Pitchoff Mountain: Monica, Francis ("Cub"), Evelyn, and Mary. Photograph by Carolyn Schaefer.

just a short way up the hill from ours. Carolyn enjoyed the simple life at the log cabin, and the lack of modern conveniences did not seem to bother her. Sometimes, she would climb a hill or mountain alone and record in her diary, "Gee, it was fun."

Thirty-five airline miles north of the cabin, Mount Marcy's summit rises a mile above the waters of Lake Champlain. This peak is near the center of the High Peaks region with more than forty mountains standing above 4,000 feet in elevation. About 200 miles of trails link many of the High Peaks, but many of them remain trail-less. The only shelter available in all of that vast region are a few open lean-tos, miles apart. Hikers must plan to sleep under the open skies and deal with the unpredictable and at times incredibly severe weather. The Adirondack Mountain Club awards the coveted "46er" pin to individuals who climb all of the High Peaks.

In 1953, Carolyn and the children decided to climb the High Peaks and become "46ers." They began an adventure that consumed the best part of four summers. The children ranged in age from seven to seventeen. I would transport them and their equipment in my old green pickup truck to a trailhead somewhere in the High Peaks, and there they would begin their trek to the summits. On the following Saturday, I would meet them at a designated place, load up their equipment in the back of the truck, and return to the log cabin. There they would feast on melons and vegetables for the rest of the weekend and prepare to take off again on Monday for another such week in the High Peaks. All of the family except me became "46ers."

Carolyn kept a journal of these trips, which the children published shortly after her death in 1985. Each of them contributed an essay, and some of the experiences they recounted are chilling. In the preface to these memoirs which she entitled *The Schaefer Expeditions*, she wrote:

> Most of our mountains were climbed in five or six
> day camping trips. For a family I think it is much better

Mary and Her Dalmatian

My daughter Mary and her Dalmatian. The dog served in the K9 Corps of the U.S. Army and its invasion forces in the South Pacific in World War II.

than rushing in to climb a mountain and rushing out. It gives your children a chance to explore the territory, climb surrounding mountains, fish and get the "feel" of the country. I loved it, myself.

It was during this period that the battle to save the Moose River country from inundation by Panther Mountain Dam reached its peak. I was barnstorming the state, often with Howard Zahniser. As we went from meeting to meeting telling audiences about the importance of wilderness and wild rivers, it gave us much satisfaction to know that our families were deeply involved with the challenges of the mountains.

The children are grown now with families and careers of their own, but the mountains continue to be a vital part of their busy lives. Our youngest, Monica, was ten when she became a "46er"; her children are now following in her footsteps. "Cub" has rock climbed extensively out west. Evelyn and Mary are always looking for new mountains and the time to climb them. Those many years of climbing mountains and hiking in Cabin Country and the High Peaks gave them the experience they needed to handle many difficult situations they would later face in life.

The Last Day

It was about noon on Sunday, the last day of trout season for the year. My son, "Cub," reminded me of a promise that I had made to go trout fishing before the end of the season. I had been working hard on the Panther Mountain dam fight and had forgotten all about it. I sensed his deep disappointment and decided to do something about it.

"If we only had some bait," I began . . .

"I've already got it," he said.

"Then get your pole and we'll go!" I replied.

We headed for the Adirondacks up the back way via the Mohawk and Sacandaga rivers. I tried to think where in thunder we could go that would give us a chance for a trout or two before the season ended that day. As we traveled over the hills of the Mohawk to Route 8 and the Sacandaga, it occurred to me that only a relatively deep pool with cold water would be likely to produce a trout of any size this late in a dry season.

I knew of one such pool near enough to a highway to reach it in the few hours we had left. It was fed by a cataract dropping off a high mountain ledge. I had not fished it for years, but it was one place we just might get a trout or two. It was a good 65 miles from home.

We reached a point in the highway several hundred yards from the pool, as I remembered it. We moved quickly from the car through the woods toward the pool. I suggested to Cub that he get his pole, line, and bait ready, out of sight of the

142

water, and walk ever so quietly to the edge of the water. He did so, obviously thrilled at this last chance for a trout.

The water was like glass. He cast to a point near the pool's center. The bait hit the water and slowly settled. All of a sudden, the water splashed, and a good-sized trout took the bait and headed for some rocks at the inlet. All I heard from Cub was a low yell as he tried to bring the fish ashore.

The fish rid itself of the hook, and Cub's line went slack. I told Cub to come back where I stood and let things settle a bit before he tried again. He was anxious to try again right away because the afternoon was slipping away. We waited fifteen minutes, and then he tried again.

He cast in near the same spot. The bait settled slowly, and again a trout struck. It did not have the same kind of action the first one did, but it was a nice-sized trout. This time, Cub landed it and came up to me with a happy smile.

I suggested to him that once again we should let the pool regain its stillness, and then I would like to try.

Shadows were lengthening when I felt it was now or never. I cast close to the inlet. Nothing happened. I tried again. No action. I began to think that Cub had caught the only trout in the pool. I decided to wait a bit and then try once more before we left.

I cast into the middle of the pool. There was an instantaneous reaction as a trout hit the bait and leapt clear of the water. This is one trout I did not lose. It was one trout that made Cub and me experience the richness of the Adirondacks. It also made me realize how shortsighted I had been to nearly deny my son an experience that would be with him always.

The trout were so beautiful in their myriad blending of orange, silver, and blue with red spots that we decided not to dress them. We packed them in ferns and placed them in the creel so Mom could see the gorgeous fish intact. We decided to have them mounted by a taxidermist.

Not long ago, Cub came in from Wyoming, where he now lives. He went into the Adirondack Room in my home in

Niskayuna and saw the two trout we had taken so many years ago hanging there on the wall. With his usual gusto, he exclaimed, "Boy, that was some day! You got the big one."

The trout were not record breakers, or even large, as Adirondack trout fishermen will say. But they were as large as we possibly could have hoped they might be that last afternoon of trout season so many years ago.

A Day in the Wilderness
with Zahnie

One afternoon during the summer in the early 1950s, Howard Zahniser dropped in at my Adirondack log cabin to renew the conversation we had started the night before at his mountainside cabin half a mile away. Howard was the executive director of the Wilderness Society in Washington, D.C., and very concerned about Adirondacks issues. He was helping us develop national strategies for our battle to save the Moose River wilderness and its virgin forest located about 40 miles to the west. We also had discussed the growing threats to wilderness everywhere by the increasing penetrations of Jeeps and planes into remote areas. I recalled when I met Bob Marshall nearly two decades earlier that even then he viewed mechanized incursions as the major threat to the integrity of the country's vanishing wilderness regions. Bob had founded the Wilderness Society, and now Howard was carrying Bob's ideals forward by crusading for a National Wilderness Preservation Act.

Because we had talked so long into the night, I asked him if he would rather take a hike into Bog Meadow. He agreed, and we head for the trail that enters the Siamese Ponds Wilderness a scant quarter-mile away. We were leaving a land that slopes gently for a couple of miles to a valley where Crane Mountain rises majestically to fill the view. Close at hand,

Flowed Lands

In 1946, Howard Zahniser, Ed Richard and I camped in a lean-to at the Flowed Lands in the High Peaks. Howard was captivated by the view of the water and mountains and remarked, "So this was Bob Marshall's country. No wonder he loved it so." With that, he took this photograph, the last on a roll of film he had with him. Bob Marshall founded the Wilderness Society and heralded the cry of wilderness preservation across the United States.

Cataract Mountain stands precipitously, its ragged spruce etched sharply against the sky. We would go about three miles before we reached Bog Meadow, a small lovely opening in an otherwise heavy forest. The meadow has been an ancient habitat for beaver, and they still occupy it perennially.

Along the trail are clumps of violets, trout lilies, trillium, and an occasional Indian pipe. The forest floor for miles in all directions is lush with ferns. We startle several deer but do not see them. A brightly colored salamander crawls along a moss-covered tree lying alongside the path. The forest's canopy almost blocks out the sky.

As we proceed, discussing the centuries-old hardwoods and the value of these protected watershed forests, we notice that the sun has vanished and the sky has become overcast. Several days of rain during the previous week had left the trail moist with an occasional pool in low spots. We cross a cold spring brook, go further, and cross another one. Their waters will not meet for 50 miles. We reach the Height-of-Land, about 2,300 feet in elevation, and follow the trail down a gentle grade into the deep woods.

We are in no hurry. For me to be with Zahnie in wilderness is an end in itself, as I had discovered about five years earlier on our first trip into the Adirondack High Peaks. All of nature seems to take on a new significance when I walk leisurely with him in this kind of country.

We reach Bog Meadow in mid-afternoon. The beavers have again built a dam on the stream. The placid waters of the little pond reflect the sky and the great trees surrounding it. I toss a grasshopper into the water and it disappears instantly as a brook trout breaks the water's surface. We sit under some balsams at the pond's edge for a while. Dragonflies dip and soar over the pond. We see an occasional bird in the treetops. All is still. It is a time when one can hear the melody of silence.

To the north of us is a swamp interspersed with an occasional hardwood hummock. Half a mile away is a tiny sheet of water I call Lost Shanty Pond. We head for it. At the pond, we startle a deer, which bounds off through the woods. Several small islands, heavy with brush and small trees, float on the still, dark waters. The islands add additional wildness to the scene. We walk around the pond, looking for some evidence of man. A footprint, a dead campfire, a piece of paper. We find none. There are an abundance of deer tracks and those of a bear. On the west side of the pond, where decades ago I took my first antlered buck, is a boulder-strewn hillside. It invites you to tarry, to sit on a rock and think, or to just sit.

Howard is to leave for Washington tomorrow, so we review again our strategy for the Moose River fight, which after five years is reaching new legal and political heights. We talk about that greatest of conservation-minded families in New York: Louis, Jim, Bob, and George Marshall. We talk about Robert Sterling Yard, Richard Westwood, and Hugh Hammond Bennett. About Ira Gabrielson, Anthony Wayne Smith, and Pinky Gutermuth, all of whom are involved in our New York conservation battles. We stop talking and listen to the absolute silence of the wilderness.

Suddenly, I realize that the afternoon has slipped away. An overcast sky has hidden the sun, and we have become unaware of the time. Dusk is falling. We have no flashlights, so we move quickly toward Bog Meadow and the trail that leads to our clearing. It is almost dark when we reach the trail.

Ten minutes later, it is so dark I cannot see my hand in front of my face. The trail is rough and rocky, depressed from the adjacent woods so that it is not too difficult to place one foot ahead of the other and make some progress. We notice something very strange on the trail. Scattered bits of a dull phosphorescent light glow in the moist parts of the trail. We kneel to examine them. Tiny mushrooms, phosphorescent! We move cautiously ahead expecting a quick end to this good fortune. But the strange glow beckons us on, and we move at a good pace for some time. At the Height-of-Land we lose the glow. We continue our pace; the trail runs almost straight down the hill to a clearing above the cabin. We see an open sky clearing of mist and Cataract Mountain looming despite the darkness.

• • •

Before the cheerful light of the cabin's fireplace, we marveled at our experience. We had both seen "foxfire" before, phosphorus in decayed wood, but this phenomena in living mushrooms was something else again. Howard and I had climbed several mountains, been caught in a violent storm atop one, and had known the joy of a deep wilderness campfire in the High Peaks. Most of our trips were under adverse conditions of one kind or another. As he got up and prepared to head for his cabin he remarked that it seemed that something wonderful happened on every trip we made. I watched him from the cabin door, playing the strong flashlight that I had forgotten earlier in the day on both sides of the trail, stopping once or twice to examine something of interest. As he disappeared in the woods, I concluded that Howard was a man who epitomized the movement to preserve the American wilderness.

Howard Zahniser

Howard Zahniser on top of Crane Mountain in 1952.

Wilderness Forever

It is a bold thing for a human being who lives on the earth for just a few score years at the most to presume upon the Eternal and covet perpetuity for any of his undertakings.

Yet we who concern ourselves with wilderness preservation are compelled to assume this boldness and with the courage of this particular undertaking of ours so to order our enterprise as to direct our efforts toward the perpetual—to project into the eternity of the future some of that precious unspoiled ecological inheritance that has come to us out of the eternity of the past.

Howard Zahniser
Wilderness Conference
San Francisco 1962

The Morehouses

Mossy Brook, a tributary of North Creek, tumbles down its boulder stream course about 100 yards from the log cabin over towards Cataract Mountain. It rises at the foot of a ledge. Its source is a spring. Several smaller streams make their way down the nearby hills above the cabin, but often in times of draught they were quite dry.

One summer's day, tired from carrying water to the cabin from Mossy Brook, I asked Johnny if he could dig a well for me. "Sartinly," he said. "I reckin I can get ye water less than a rod down. Right here under this maple. See that thar limb, bendin down towards the ground? Points to water."

Two weeks later, I came up for the weekend. The well was dug! It was about 3 feet in diameter between the stones he used to encircled it. It was almost 12 feet deep and had 3 feet of ice-cold water. I took a draft from a pail we dropped into it. It was crystal clear and sweet. I was delighted and told him so.

"D'y'ee see anything ya don't lak about it?," he asked.

"Not a thing," I replied. "How much do I owe you?"

"Wal," he said. "It was quite a job. Had to use dynamite, too. Is twenty dollars too much?"

Even in those days, when a dollar was really a dollar, it seemed awfully cheap. I happened to have that much on me, and I gave it to him.

"Are ya sure you're satisfied? Ya don't see anything wrong?," he asked. I nodded.

"Then I hev ta tell ya. Look up in the tree. The dynamite blowed off thet big limb, and I was afeared ya wouldn't like it." He looked at me questionably. Only then did I realize how much I must have been talking about trees to these mountain men.

Later, I asked Johnny's son George to build me a stone topping above the well so we could cover it. Then we added a well-sweep which has been renewed several times as time moves relentlessly onward.

The well has been a blessing for all of us and for the many hunters who have stopped by the side of the trail for a draft of Johnny's water.

• • •

On one October morning about 1930, I decided it was about time to put a larger window in the south side of the cabin in order that I could better enjoy the brilliant fall colors on the mountain. The flaming scarlet of the maples, the gold of the popples, and the myriad colors of other trees, plus the deep black of the spruce and balsam at skyline was a sight to behold. It would be fine, I thought, to have that view while eating breakfast.

Johnny came over when he heard me pounding and sawing the logs. When he saw what I was doing, he remarked, "Ya're gonna be cold this winter. Logs is warmer than glass."

The next week I brought up the window and installed it. Johnny came over again. The sun had created a kaleidoscope of color too gorgeous to describe. He sat at the table and looked out. It was warm. I lifted the sash and hooked it above. A fresh cool breeze wafted in from the wilderness. "Ya did alroight m'by. Guess I'll do something like thet," Johnny said.

The next day, on my way home, I stopped by his home to say good-bye. "I'll bring you up a window next week," I told him.

"Don't need ta, b'ye. It's all done. See?"

I went into his house and sure enough, there on the south-

Johnny Morehouse   George Morehouse

west side, facing the mountain was a window already installed. He went over to it and rolled it down and then up again.

I was flabbergasted!

He had ripped a door off an old sedan not far away and spiked it to the side of his house. He then rolled down the window and cut a hole in the wall! It was in some ways, more practical than mine!

In a small clearing hard up against a mountain wilderness where a cold crystal stream splashed over boulders in a small ravine, a tiny hut was built into a sand hill. It was camouflaged with logs and earth so as to be almost invisible. Into this

Doug Morehouse

Arthur Morehouse

setting was a mountaineer who occasionally had a thirst for "spirits."

Johnny was the mountaineer. The hut was on log cabin property which he still owned. He had excavated an area about 10 by 12 feet and covered it with logs, dirt, and leaves. It was about 6 feet high inside and had been built during the days of prohibition, about 1924. Where Johnny learned to make "spirits" I'll never know, for I never asked him. He had a copper kettle and pipe and whatever else a still requires to distill alcohol.

One fall day, two hunters came out of the woods in bedraggled condition and told Johnny, who was hoeing potatoes, that they had become lost and had come out miles from where they had begun their hunt. Johnny offered them food...flapjacks and syrup and tea. "All we want is a little liquor," they said. "We'll pay anything for it."

"Can't help you boys with that," Johnny said.

"But we must have a shot of liquor," they repeated.

With this, Johnny melted and told them he'd give them a touch of it but not for pay. "Follow me," he told them. They went over to his underground room, and Johnny gave them each a small portion of liquor in an old tin cup.

Then the hunters opened the lapel of their coats and displayed the badge of a federal law enforcement agency. "You are under arrest," they informed the dumbfounded Johnny.

The next day, the city newspapers carried headlines: "Huge Mountain Still Discovered" and "Adirondack Native Faces Serious Charges."

Our whole family was shocked. Here was the man who had enriched our lives, giving us milk and eggs and potatoes and even berries. Here was our good samaritan in trouble with the law. Here was a man who never knew anything but freedom threatened with a jail cell.

A hunting party from East Greenbush, New York, who had been guided by Johnny heard of it and arranged for his bail. The trial was scheduled for federal court in Albany. Letters were sent to Governor Alfred E. Smith. The most notable letter I am sure came from my mother, who explained to him that Johnny had made life bearable in the face of financial shortages each summer, had helped her regain her health, kept her family together, and herself out of a sanitarium. He had done what no one else could.

Several months later, Johnny stood before a federal judge in the Albany courtroom. He was in his native mountain garb, clean and bearded, and respectful in these august surroundings.

The judge read the charge.

"Guilty or not guilty?" the judge asked.

"I reckin," said Johnny, "I did what you said I did."

There was a murmuring in the courtroom. The judge left the room for a few moments and then returned to his rostrum.

He admonished the mountaineer.

"You have broken the law," he said. "You must desist."

"Yes, sir," said Johnny.

"I fine you one dollar and costs," he said.

There were sighs of relief. The hunters embraced him. A grateful Johnny went back to his mountains and did as he was told. The copper kettle and bits of pipe are still to be found at that site along the brook.

• • •

Leo Franklin lived across the street from our home in Bellevue during the late 1920s. He was a metal spinner at the General Electric Research Laboratory and an excellent mechanic. At that time he was about thirty-five years old, and I was about twenty. Although I had never met him, I used to see him returning from fishing or hunting trips. His dad and mine were close friends.

One afternoon during July, he came across the street to the porch where I was sitting. "My dad says that you have a cabin up in trout country," he said. I told him that was correct and proceeded as always to enthuse about it.

"Any chance to go up there sometime fishing?," he asked.

"Sure, " I said, "Anytime."

"How soon?"

"Tonight, if you could go," I replied.

An hour later we were in his open Dodge touring car headed for Cabin Country. Two hours later, we were sitting in front of our blazing fireplace planning a trip for the morrow.

I suggested that we go back into the wilderness to Tombstone Swamp about four miles to the west. Second Pond Brook coursed its serpentine way through an ancient beaver meadow there. Several years earlier, I had noticed a stone about 6 inches square and 3 feet above the ground along an old game trail on its western bank. I had no idea what it represented and had never found anyone who did. I named the meadow.

We were up at dawn and headed up along the trail to Bog Meadow, which passes the cabin door. Shortly, we were in a heavy forest predominantly hardwood with occasional hemlocks and spruce. The trail climbed a ridge and then undulated its twisting course for several miles to a point near Bog Meadow. Here, we left the trail and struck across the pathless woods to the swamp, about a mile and a half distant. The cool of the morning soon became a very hot and muggy day. We passed Lost Shanty Pond and then dropped over a ridge to Tombstone.

We had lunch there and started fishing. The water was low, and the trout were not hitting. The day was so hot that we decided to rest in the shade of some spruce, then head downstream to The Flow, and fish the stream during the late afternoon. The day was spent by the time we reached the best part of the stream, the junction of a cold spring brook with the main stream. The sun was beginning to color mackerel clouds and cast increasingly bright crimson colors on the waters.

Never before had either of us seen the way the trout were hitting that day. They leapt for our lures and sometimes got nothing more than the bare hook. It was obvious from the first that we would keep only the larger ones. That meant a foot or more in length. We released many smaller ones.

The beavers had built a small dam a hundred or more yards below this stream junction. Standing on the dam, the fishing equaled the best that we had. In a short time our creels were full, and the trout cleaned and packed in moss and ferns. We headed for the clearing, reaching there at dusk. We hung our creels in the well and repaired to the cabin to relive the day.

The next morning, it was still unusually hot. It was to be another scorcher. We decided to try to find some ice on the way home to preserve the freshness of our catch. We left the cabin about ten o'clock in the morning and headed down the road toward Baker's Mills. About half a mile on our way there was a sudden snap of metal, and the car stopped. Leo looked at me with eyes that indicated a disaster. "It sounded like a gear in the transmission," he said.

Leo was an expert mechanic. After blocking the wheels, he got under the transmission at the rear end. In minutes the plate was off, and the problem evident. "It's the spider gear," he said. "We'll never find anything like that up in this country. This is a real disaster. And our trout. . . . "

There was a movement on the bank above the car. There stood Doug Morehouse, who lived close by and who was the acknowledged leader of the guides in this area. He was a tall and distinguished man. He guided parties from far places to his hunting camp tents at The Flow. His success ratio was high.

"What's the trouble, boys?," he asked. From under the car Leo held a piece of the broken gear. Then, as I remember it, he took off a wheel, pulled out an axle, and picked the gear out of the transmission case. He handed it to Doug. Doug turned it over in his hand slowly, contemplating the broken metal.

"I'm not sure, but I think I know where there is one like this. I'll be right back," he mumbled. He headed back up and across his fields towards a stone wall near a brook. I had known that whenever someone found a piece of metal in a field that they would put it on a stone wall or fence. This was true even in the Mohawk Valley, where I was familiar with the practice.

Twenty minutes later, Doug was back at our car and asked Leo if what he wanted was something like this rusty thing. And he handed it to Leo.

Leo was speechless. He got out his wallet and opened it up to a number of bills. He offered it to Doug. "Whatever you want, its yours," he said. "This is unreal. It's impossible. I can't believe I'm awake."

"No way, son," he said. "It's yours. Maybe someday you can do something for a body that needs it," Doug replied. He stayed there until Leo had replaced the gear, took the stones away from the wheels, and shook hands with him. We were soon on our way. We soon had ice in our creels. Leo never got over that experience. And neither have I, although sixty years have passed since that day.

• • •

In the early days, I often hitchhiked to the cabin for a weekend hunt. On one such occasion, I had hunted so long and hard that when Sunday night came I was too tired to think about the long trip home even though I was due at work the next morning. I asked Arthur Morehouse (Doug Morehouse's son), who lived down the road, if he would take me to North Creek the next morning so I could catch the 6:00 A.M. train to Saratoga. Because I would be late for work, I asked him to be sure to get me to the station on time. He assured me I had no worry about that.

It was still dark that cold morning when I heard Arthur blow the bulbous horn on his old Model T Ford. I grabbed my pack and ran from the cabin to Johnny Morehouse's yard, where Arthur was waiting for me. "The radiator leaks; we'll have to stop on the way," he said. And off we went down the hill toward Baker's Mills with a roar and a clatter.

I sat in the front with Arthur. The car had no top and no windshield, but it did have a generous amount of polished brass visible. The radiator and cap were brass. A light fixture on the driver's side was brass. From it hung a 10-quart pail with what was obviously a handmade brass handle. I wondered what the pail was for. "The radiator leaks a little," he told me. "But no problem."

All roads in that country were dirt in those days. When we came to Baker's Mills, where a sharp left-hand turn was required, we seemed to make it on two wheels. Weaving in and out on the twisting road toward North Creek, we were making great time. As we came to a brook that crossed the road, Arthur stopped suddenly, using the reverse gears to do so. He jumped out, got a pail of water, and poured it in the radiator. Then we took off again in another cloud of dust. I began to worry about getting to the station in time and said so.

"If you don't stop worrying, we probably won't make it," he rejoined. So, I kept still until we came to the next brook running beside the road. Once again he stopped and filled the radiator. And again we took off in a cloud of dust. Knowing it was questionable if we could reach there in time, Art gave the car all the gas it would take. I'll never forget the rest of that ride. I hung on for dear life, my hair was blowing wildly in the wind, as I started to think up excuses to tell my boss for missing not only one day's work but probably two. We came in sight of the village and roared down the main street toward the railroad station. (It was the same one that Teddy Roosevelt reached early one morning after President McKinley was assassinated, there to find himself president of the nation.)

The engine was belching steam. Attached to it was a coal tender, a baggage car, and a passenger car. The conductor saw us pull up and stepped off the car, motioned to the engineer to hold, and waved us in. Arthur carried my pack in and I my rifle. I breathlessly told the conductor that I had no ticket.

"You can pay me," he said. Arthur put my pack on a seat and jumped off the car. I was the only passenger. The conductor closed the door, the engineer tooted the whistle once, and we began to move.

The conductor sat across from me and asked me questions about the hunt, the country, and all the rest. I don't remember what I told him, but our conversation lasted quite a while as we moved with increasing speed down along the Hudson River, which wound south through forested mountains.

As the miles rolled past us and conversation stopped, I began to vaguely remember stories I had heard of wealthy people, in the past century, building their own railroad into the wilderness and riding there on specially designed coaches, replete with a cook and a maid. I began to realize, as I sat there enjoying the river scenery, that all they had that I didn't have on this particular day was a cook and a maid.

Old Log Cabin

The old log cabin before we planted the plantation with a view of Crane Mountain in the distance.

The Plantations

Below the log cabin was a field. It was full of boulders, scant in soil, and supported sparse grass and goldenrod. It sloped gently to the east toward a valley two miles away and granted a magnificent view of Crane Mountain.

In 1931, I decided to reforest the land. The experts at the New York State tree nursery at Saratoga suggested that I plant spruce and red pine. I ordered 5,000 trees, and I picked them up for ten dollars in the early spring. I had discussed the idea with Johnny, and he was incredulous. "M'by," he said, "Trees is meant to cut, not ta plant. Ye'll spile the view my father made."

When my brother Carl and I showed him the 5,000 seedlings that I could easily hold in my two hands, he scoffed. "Trees," he remonstrated. "Why them things ain't hardly bin born yet." Reluctantly, he agreed to plant them after we showed him how with a mattock. He would have Carl and a neighbor, Willie, help him.

The next Friday afternoon, I was at Johnny's door. "Did you get the trees planted?" I asked him. "Why sartinly," he said. "Can't ya see how they've already shet into the sun?" It had started to rain.

The next day, I walked across the "plantation." Only here and there, among the weeds, could I find a tiny transplant. I began to think I was a fool to think a forest would result.

For several years, it was almost impossible to find the

A Cabin in the Making

Fifty years after I planted the plantation of spruce and pine, my friends Dan and Noel Johnson used some of the trees to build one of the finest log cabins in the Adirondack Park. I designed it for them, and it faces Crane Mountain.

trees, except on a small sandy hill over by the creek where even weeds would not grow. It was that hill that made me decide I was no farmer. But strangely, the trees were growing well there.

During the next years, my conservation activities kept me so busy that I used the cabin only to sleep in and did not roam the land. When I did notice that trees were springing up all over the place, I got some more and established four more plantations of smaller size.

The years rolled on, and the trees began to prosper. Soon, they were as tall as I was, then 10 feet, 15 feet, 30 feet, and more in height. I found that Johnny was right. The splendid view of Crane Mountain was gone.

My conservation activities kept me from thinking about the plantations until one winter's day, with snow heavy on all the branches, I finally perceived that I did indeed have a forest—as a matter of fact, five of them. The trees just kept growing a foot or more each year until when they were 85 feet high. I realized they were fine enough to build a log cabin.

In the early 1980s, I gave friends of mine trees enough to build what is one of the finest log cabins in the Adirondack Park. As Carl and I watched it go up, log upon log, ceiling beams, fireplace mantels, and rafters, we could hardly believe that once they were trees not larger than a wooden pencil that we held in our hands.

After the trees had been cut for the cabin, their loss was not even noticeable in the plantations where all manner of natural things have come to life—canoe birches more than a foot in diameter, princess pine, snows that linger into June, deer grouse, fox, woodchucks, and snowshoe rabbits. The view is gone, and we have to climb the hill to see the mountain as we once did. In its place is an infinity of nature that has grown rapidly within my lifetime.

Cave on Crane Mountain

*Blackened rocks of campfires built by Jeanne Robert Foster still re-
main on the floor of this cave on Crane Mountain. Notice that the
sliding rock has bent the trees. Photograph by Dan Ling.*

Jeanne Robert Foster

During our ten-year battle to save the Moose River Country from devastation by reservoirs that began in 1945, the Adirondack Moose River Committee received several small checks from a woman named Jeanne Robert Foster. With each check came a note saying that no acknowledgment was necessary and to keep up the good fight.

In 1968, we were working to block the proposed Gooley dam on the Upper Hudson River. This inundation would have destroyed 35 miles of forest in the geographical center of the Adirondack Park. This time, the Adirondack Hudson River Association, received a check from Jeanne Robert Foster with the same note on it.

Because she lived in Schenectady I called her to express my thanks for her numerous contributions and continued support. The conversation soon led to Crane Mountain. I explained to her that Crane was "my mountain," and I was surprised she had not asked my permission to climb it. She immediately responded, "There was a very good reason. I was guiding touristers up that mountain when I was ten years old and living at the Putnam farm at the base of it. That was some years before you were born." I was dumbfounded. I had to know more about this woman.

By some strange coincidence I found that an acquaintance of mine, Ruth Riedinger, knew Jeanne Robert Foster quite well. She invited me join her and her children, Noel and Theodore, when they went to visit Jeanne the following Christmas Eve. I went to Crane, cut a small balsam tree, and arrived that evening with tree in hand.

I found Jeanne to be a friendly, delightful, scholarly woman in her early eighties. Her home was filled with books and art, plus memorabilia from some of the literary and artistic greats of the world—John Butler Yeats, his son William Butler Yeats, Ezra Pound, James Joyce, Constantin Brancuşi, Ford Madox Ford, André Derain, and others. I found that she had been a close friend of John Quinn, a patron of many writers and artists and an art collector. Jeanne had lived in New York City for a number of years before she returned to Schenectady during the Great Depression.

As I talked with her, I found that she had been born in the Adirondacks into the Putnam family that settled at the base of Crane Mountain along Mill Creek Road. When she was young, she had been farmed out to her uncle, Rev. Francis Putnam (Elliot Putnam's father) and lived with his family for a couple of years on his farm several miles back in the woods off the main road. It was from here she took touristers up the mountain for twenty-five cents and in the process fell in love with this geologic massif. She never lost her love for the mountain despite her worldwide travels and her association with many of the great literary and artistic people in the 1920s.

I learned also that while she lived in New York she had been an assistant to John Agar. Agar was president of the influential Association for the Protection of the Adirondacks and worked in cooperation with Governor Alfred E. Smith to block the proposed Salmon River dam, which would have obliterated much of the best deer wintering grounds in the northern Adirondacks.

Jeanne asked me if I knew of the cave near the lake on the lower summit of Crane Mountain. I did not. She told me how to find it; and soon thereafter, I found on the cliff wall the blackened rocks of campfires she had lit so many decades ago.

During the years from that initial meeting with her until

Crane Mountain Pond

The summit of Crane Mountain lifts above the pond high on the mountain. Photograph by Dan Ling.

her death in 1970, we corresponded fairly regularly. She was one of the few people who shared my spiritual relationship with Crane Mountain. In her book, *Adirondack Portraits: A Piece of Time*, edited by Noel Riedinger-Johnson and published by Syracuse University Press in 1986 and quoted by permission, she describes the mountain:

Crane Mountain
(for Paul Schaefer)

How can I lift my mountain before your eyes,
Tear it out of my heart, my hands, my sinews,
Lift it before you—its trees, its rocks,
Its thrust heavenward;
The basic cliffs, the quartz of the outcrop,
The wide water in the cup of the lower summit,
The high peak lifting above the timberline
Gathering the mist of fifty lakes at sunrise;
The waterfall tumbling a thousand feet,
White with foam, white with rock-flower in summer;
The wreathing of dark spruce and hemlock,
The blood splashes of mountain ash,
The long spur to the north golden with poplars;
A porcupine drinking, bending without fear
To his image?
When darkness shall by my home,
Eternal mountain, do not leave my heart;
Remain with me in my sleep,
In my dreams, in my resurrection.

By another strange quirk of fate, the historic Putnam farm was purchased by a group of youngsters, including several of my children. The outlet of the lake drops into meadows of the farm exactly the way Jeanne describes it in her poem.

It was at the farmhouse that I met Elliot Putnam on January 28, 1931, on my way to the top of the mountain in sub-zero weather. He asked me to stay overnight and climb in the morning. When I persisted in going on, he hung a lantern on his house in case I returned. He asked me to give a hounding call if and when I reached the trail near the lake. This I did; and this handsome, spare, blue-eyed retired preacher responded from the valley 1,000 feet below.

Adirondack Cooking Crane

Adirondack Cooking Crane

In mid-August of 1953, I reached the cabin about noon and took off with creel and fish pole to The Flow, about four miles back in the woods. I took no lunch because I had a fine steak waiting for me. I returned about four o'clock, ravenously hungry, and prepared a fire in the fireplace to cook the steak and brew some coffee. I placed a grill atop two rocks, placed the steak where it would cook slowly, and set the coffee pot nearby. While I sat in front of the fireplace savoring my meal, I took a book from a nearby shelf to pass the time. All of a sudden, the coffee pot boiled over. I grabbed, and coffee spilled over the steak and doused the fire.

The air in my cabin was blue for a while. A little hound I had never seen before stood in the doorway with a questioning attitude. Without thinking, I tossed the coffee-clad steak to him, and he ran off with it, his tail wagging wildly. How ridiculous to cook a meal in an open fireplace? Was there no better way than I used? The old-fashioned fireplace crane was better, but what about pots and pans that could not hang from hooks? An idea came to me: I could hang a flat iron grill from the crane and retain the basic colonial design.

Back in Schenectady, I sketched the idea. The next morning I was at my blacksmith's shop early. When I showed him the sketch, he said he would have a prototype ready in a day or two. The next weekend, I again traveled north and gave the first cooking crane to the Zahnisers to try in their fireplace.

After a few refinements, the blacksmith and I finally had what I wanted. I had a little card designed and printed and sent one to many friends. The first reply came from Arthur C. Parker, former archaeologist of the New York State Museum at Albany, who said, "The beauty of your crane is that it looks as if it were a fitting part of the ingle nook period, but it is more than looks for it makes the old-fashioned crane more than doubly useful."

I sent the sketch to a patent attorney in Washington, D.C. In a short time, a U.S. patent was granted, and the "Adirondack Cooking Crane" went into manufacture and distribution.

The Land Nobody Knows

A group of us were in the Adirondack Room one night in 1972. The Adirondack documentary film *Of Rivers and Men* was completed. It had done its job: after Governor Nelson Rockefeller and his successor Governor Hugh Carey had seen it at the capitol, historic legislation creating a Wild, Scenic, and Recreational Rivers System had been signed, which protected 1,200 miles of rivers in the Adirondack Park. We were trying to decide what we should do next.

The people at the meeting offered all kinds of suggestions. We read the first paragraph in the two volume *History of the Adirondacks*, which was published in 1921 when the park was somewhat smaller than at present. A portion of the paragraph read: "The Adirondacks are a group of mountains in north-eastern New York. . . . There are about one hundred peaks ranging 1,200 feet to 5,000 feet in height." On the wall was the 12-foot-high scaled relief map of the Adirondacks made from the U.S. Geological Survey maps. On that map there were over two thousand mountains! We all admitted that we—like the author of the earlier book—knew very little about these mountains. We decided that night to make a 16-mm film entitled *The Adirondack—The Land Nobody Knows*. We formed the Couch-sa-chra-ga Association to produce the film.

We invited two excellent cinematographers, Walter Haas and Edwin Niedhammer, to our first meeting. They agreed to photograph and to do anything else they could to produce the

175

Cinematographers

Cinematographers Walter Haas and Edwin Niedhammer on the West River in the Silver Lake Wilderness.

film. Others offered to pack equipment and be of help in any-way possible. All volunteered their services.

We decided to include footage of Cabin Country and our wilderness hunting camp. Ed and Walt filmed our teamster hauling in our tents and equipment to our favored part of the Siamese Ponds Wilderness. Around the table that night our hunters admitted that they had seen not more than four of the sixty-seven lakes in this one wilderness, although they had hunted the region for decades. There are fifteen such wilder-ness areas, some much larger than this one. Walt and Ed got a good idea that night of how little is really known about much of the park.

For more than six years, Walt, Ed, and I crisscrossed the park with cameras and tripods. We spent every weekend year round and most of our vacations there. Frequently, we would travel four hundred miles on a two-day trip to find that most people we talked to knew very little about the park except for the particular section they lived in or favored. We climbed mountains, slept in the wilderness, and photographed rampag-ing rivers, great forests, and wildlife. Walt's and Ed's skills, dedication, and determination showed in the excellent images they captured on film. Some of our hunters served as packers and guides. Many times, other skilled cinematographers and naturalists living in the park assisted us in getting specific foot-age needed to produce a well-balanced film.

The script for the film was written by Noel Riedinger-Johnson. She spent a year working full time to edit the five miles of film that the men in the field shot. She was helped extensively by Anne Wait, Carolyn Hatch, and Libby Smith. She also designed the graphics and arranged for Betsy Blades-Zeller to compose the film's original music score. All postproduction and technical aspects of the film were carried out under her direction. Jack O'Field served as technical consultant.

Members of our new association, led by Winifred LaRose of Lake George, sent out thousands of letters to raise the addi-

Cine

The Council on International Nontheatrical Events
congratulates

Couch-sa-chra-ga Association, Inc.

for the motion picture

**The Adirondack—
The Land Nobody Knows**

Produced by an Amateur Film Maker and

selected for its excellence to represent the

United States of America in international

motion picture events abroad and awards to it

PRESIDENT

The Cine Eagle

© 1962 by CINE

Cine Eagle Award

*The film won a Cine Eagle Award and was chosen to represent the
United States in international film competitions. It not only won a
major award in Los Angeles but also won awards throughout the
world in such places as Canada, Spain, Portugal, Malta, and New
Zealand.*

tional money needed to supplement the grants given by the New York State Council on the Arts, the Association for the Protection of the Adirondacks, the American Conservation Association, and the New York State Conservation Council. American Motors lent us a Jeep, and Dick Weber contributed thousands of dollars worth of helicopter time to enable Ed to get dynamic aerial shots.

As the film gradually took shape under the skillful direction of Noel, the question of a first showing came up in late 1979. We were asked to premiere the film at the Egg in the Empire State Mall in Albany. Mayor Erastus Corning, Environmental Conservation Commissioner Robert Flacke, and Transportation Commissioner William Hennessy were to be the hosts. More than five hundred individuals from across the nation attended the opening on February 9, 1980.

We were not prepared for the fine reception the film received. The Washington-based Council on International Nontheatrical Events awarded the film its Cine Eagle and offered to enter it in film festivals here and abroad. The film received high awards throughout the world in such places as Los Angeles, Canada, Portugal, Spain, Malta, and New Zealand. It was also selected as one of the top six amateur films produced in the United States in 1980. In New York State fifty-two educational services in all upstate counties, ten regional library systems, and eleven universities purchased copies of it for their libraries. Many state agencies and innumerable organizations did likewise. Recently, the film was converted to video tape, and more than a hundred videos have been sold.

One of the most significant reviews came from the American Association for the Advancement of Science. M. John Loeffer of Colorado had this to say in a statement that went to five thousand film centers:

> The Adirondack Mountains, the southernmost tip of the Canadian Shield, are depicted in this film as a constitutionally protected area of upper New York State. The narration and filming

meaningfully reveal the gradual evolution of landscape as the endogenic and exogenic energies wind, water, ice and gravity mold the land of hard crystalline bedrock. The central unit of the mountains is the watershed for New York State. The water harvest is excellently depicted as it is influenced by the entire blend of the biosphere, hydrosphere and lithosphere. The human incursion of the lumberjack and the ravages of fire affected the fragile ecological balance and led to management procedures. These management efforts assure a well balanced pragmatic use of the land for lumber and water power, as well as the myriad of recreational activities in proximity to intense population concentrations. Set aside by law, Adirondack State Park is an escape from the mechanistic civilization and provides a superb glimpse of the past for future generations. The film has excellent chronology and design with a well and timely phased narration. It has good information and excellent photography. Viewing this film is a good learning experience for the very young to the old.

Reflections

Paul at Beaver House

As I sit on the porch at Beaver House, I think about the wonderful years I have spent in Cabin Country. I have had an incredible life! Photograph by Paul Grondahl.

Before World War II, the old log cabin was my castle, the mountaineers and the wilderness my joy. I began my apprenticeship as a carpenter in 1923, and finished the required four years in 1927 without getting a raise in pay. The pay was meager, not much more than a token, but it helped me share the cost of the cabin and seven acres with my brother Vincent. During those early years I had almost exclusive use of the cabin. My friends with cars made trips almost weekly affairs because they enjoyed hunting and fishing.

Then the lands around the cabin were open, boulder-strewn fields. By 1931, my brother Carl and I had planted spruce and red pine seedlings in the fields below the cabin. As I mentioned earlier, Johnny Morehouse warned me that I was going to spoil the magnificent view of Crane Mountain, and before long he proved right. Members of the Mohawk Valley Hiking Club helped to plant trees on the highland meadows half a mile behind the cabin. Those seedlings are now approaching 100 feet in height and are part of the Siamese Ponds Wilderness.

During the Great Depression in the 1930s the hiking club attracted a number of scientists and engineers from the General Electric Company in Schenectady. They became involved in the club's activities that included trips to Cabin Country and other wilderness regions in the park. It was during this time that many of us met John Apperson. Apperson was an eminent Adirondack conservationist. He quickly convinced us that a way to help preserve the wild-forest character of the Adirondacks was to photograph and produce motion pictures illustrating problems threatening the mountains. We did this. Wherever we went, we had cameras with us. The hiking club was vital in the production of films that Apperson used to win important conservation battles in 1931 and 1932.

For me, these trips began adventures that shaped the rest of my life. During one of these trips to film the destruction of forests in the High Peaks region for Apperson, I met Bob Marshall on top of Mount Marcy. He saw first hand the extensive lumbering of virgin forests on Mount Adams. Not long afterward, Marshall established the Wilderness Society and penned statements about wilderness that inspired me (and countless other people in years to come). His words, "the universe of wilderness all over the United States is vanishing with appalling rapidity . . . melting away like the last snowbank on some south-facing mountain on a hot afternoon in June," along with the words of the "forever wild" covenant in the New York State Constitution became indelibly inscribed in my mind.

I used to roam the hills above the cabin and look out over the most extensive and beautiful views. Most beautiful of all was the John Dalaba farm at the end of the road. Here, he had cleared substantial acreage up to the edge of the wilderness and established a genuine mountain farm overlooking the graceful Crane Mountain and miles of hills and valleys that ended only in far horizons. I used to wander across the highlands behind his house and barn and look for woodchucks, foxes, and deer. The splendor of the view from those untillable hills remains with me. Many times, I lingered there to watch the sun burn red behind the mountains and left only when chased by impending darkness.

In those days, the hardwood forest behind the cabin was on the thin side. The large maples had been spared because of their much-needed sap. An occasional small clearing and the ever-present apple trees and lilac bushes gave evidence of pioneer log cabins. The thin soil and short growing seasons discouraged farming.

After my early hunting successes earned me a place helping mountain guides and their hunting parties, I thought that, because I had a cabin with a mountain brook running through it, I might be able to make a living like some of these mountain people did. By the brook was a sand hill that I figured might produce a harvest of potatoes. I planted a pail of potato eyes and confidently waited for nature to yield my basic winter food. When the growing season was over, my harvest was a pail of spuds not much bigger than marbles. Then and there, I decided that it would take someone more determined than I to make a living in this mountain country. I knew that I would probably do better as a carpenter.

During the depression years, our wilderness hunting began in earnest. Last year marked the fifty-eighth year we hauled tents and equipment miles back to our favored campsite. The hunts lured us to the hills and highest mountains, up and down precipices, and into almost impenetrable swamps. Hunting taught us a lot about wilderness and the intelligence of it inhabitants. It also brought together people we would not have met and bonded lasting relationships.

Except for occasional lumbering operations on private lands and the mining of garnet near North Creek, there was very little commercial activity in the Adirondacks before World War II. The Adirondack Park was a land of hamlets and villages connected by dirt roads. Few changes were made from one year to another. Hunting, fishing, and outdoor recreation were the important activities. Lake George, Lake Placid, and a few other places with their tourist attractions were the exception to the rule. Land was cheap, and New York State was steadily adding land to the forest preserve.

World War II came and things changed. A vital mineral needed for the war was titanium. Submarines threatened the main world supply from India. Another major source was found in the Tahawas region of the Adirondacks, and the federal government moved in to get it: highways were improved, a railroad built through the wilderness, a town moved, a mountain leveled, and a region of great beauty devastated.

Right after the war, Jeeps and half-tracks penetrated extensive regions of wilderness that had never known motorized equipment. The Army Corps of Engineers proposed power dams on the Moose River. Legislators proposed constitutional amendments to permit mining, cabin colonies, and other commercial activities on state lands. Maps showed a series of reservoirs planned that would inundate major game-abundant lowlands.

One day, Apperson came to the log cabin. We sat and talked about what had happened to the Adirondacks in the past and how difficult it would be to retain the wild-forest character of the mountains in the future. I knew when he left that any complacency that I might have had at that time was to be part of me no longer. The amount of time I had set aside previously to work on conservation issues would no longer be sufficient. The challenge was clear, and I would have to reorder my life to meet it.

By 1945, I had become deeply immersed in conservation battles. Ed Richard, myself, and others had begun a battle to save some of the finest forests and lowlands in the Adirondacks from being devastated by power reservoirs. The South Branch of the Moose River, the Indian and Red rivers, and numerous glacial lakes were involved, as well as the fabled Moose River Plains, the largest winter-yarding grounds for white-tailed deer in the northeast.

During that same year, Howard Zahniser expressed a desire to own a cabin in the Adirondack Park after he, Ed Richard, and I camped at the Flowed Lands in the High Peaks. He knew that Bob Marshall, founder of the Wilderness Society, began his career in the Adirondacks. The Adirondacks were Bob's favorite country, and Howard wanted to be part of it. He soon owned a fine little cabin at the end of Edward's Hill Road, just beyond the old log cabin. He joined us in the Moose River fight and enlisted important forces in Washington to assist us in the conflict that was to last ten years before it was settled in the United States Supreme Court.

In 1952, Howard arranged to have the annual council meeting of the Wilderness Society gather at my log cabin and my father's camp. From these cabins, the members of the council would go to meetings in various parts of the park. It was then that I decided to think about better facilities to accommodate these conservationists. Also, the growing families of my brothers and sisters as well as my own added importance to this thought.

One day I walked with Don Hall, a hunting friend, over the land above the log cabin to locate a site for the new cabin. We found one about halfway between the old log cabin and Zahniser's cabin. It had a fine view of the mountains. I decided to build a cabin similar to the wing I had added to my home in Niskayuna. The wing, which we called the Adirondack Room, was framed with huge, ancient Dutch hand-hewn beams, a great fireplace, an open-gable ceiling, loft, and plank floors.

Shortly afterwards, I received a call from the owner of a salvage company in Albany that had been furnishing me with beams, slate, and other such material for the traditional Dutch-design homes I specialized in building. He said he had to demolish a small building on Sanders Avenue in Albany that was "older than the hills," according to the best information he could get. I was immediately interested because, years before, I was "farmed out" to my grandfather's house on Sanders Avenue while my mother was hospitalized.

The house was indeed old. There was no key for the door, and we entered through a shuttered window. It was a small building, perhaps 20-by-30 feet. It really was ancient and looked it with cobwebs everywhere and no indication of anyone having been in it for ages. There were many fine hand-hewn beams about 8-by-10 inches and up to 20 feet in length. They were exactly what I needed for the new cabin. He told me that the people who owned it called it the "beaver house."

The house was located on the hills south of the city and about a mile or so from the Hudson River. Records show that in 1690 taxes were paid on 80,000 beaver skins shipped from Albany to Europe for the making of the celebrated "beaver hat." Some weeks later, it dawned on me that the empty vats we had seen at the house might have had something to do with beaver. When I began to clean the beams with a power sander and sensed a sweet musty odor coming from the wood, I was

Beaver House
Photograph by Dave Gibson.

convinced that the house was a part of that early export business in Albany. From this questionable evidence, I decided to call the new cabin "Beaver House."

I usually had several homes under construction during the year. My involvement with the battles over dams in the Adirondacks was taking almost all of my time when I was not on the job with the dozen or more craftsman who worked for me. I knew that building a new cabin would have to fit into that schedule. Several days a week, I would leave Schenectady about four in the afternoon, drive seventy-five miles, and work until dark on the cabin. Except for lifting the big beams in place and framing the roof, I worked alone or with my brother Carl.

After months of hard work, Beaver House was livable. The huge fireplace and the old timbers made it attractive. I had thought of it as being something of a hospice between my home and the simple life we knew in wilderness tents. It never occurred to me to make the little building as sophisticated as the fine homes I was constructing in the city. Rather, it was a place for occasional overnight stays, a gathering place for hunters on their way into the wilderness, and a place for conservationists to plan strategies for the continuing battles to retain the wild-forest character of the Adirondacks. It was the only building I ever built without a slate roof, and I did not want to worry about freezing water or plowed driveways. It was intended to be just a simple little Adirondack cabin on the edge of the wilderness, a refuge from the hustle and bustle of the life that I was living, a place to sit in front of the fireplace, alone or with friends, anticipating the trip on the morrow or reliving the adventures of the day.

• • •

As I sit here on the porch of Beaver House surrounded by mountains and forests, I think back over the years before and since this cabin was built. Except for hunting each fall, most of my time and energy centered on conservation battles. My Cabin Country expanded to include the entire Adirondack Park. My mountain adventures often occurred in legislative halls, on legislative commissions' fact-finding field trips, and at public hearings.

I found that the experiences I had with Apperson gave the background I needed for the new threats to the mountains. In 1931 and 1932 Apperson had my conversation committee of the Mohawk Valley Hiking Club distribute a pamphlet he wrote advocating the enlargement of the park. At that time Lake George, Schroon Lake, Sacandaga Reservoir, and thousands of acres above Lake Placid were not included in the park. A contitutional amendment had passed the legislature twice that would permit the state to lumber lands in these regions. Apperson had mapped the land he thought should be in the park and had secured former governor Alfred E. Smith's support. Smith and then-governor Franklin D. Roosevelt were both running for the presidency of the United States. Their opposing positions on the boundary of the park proved to be politically significant. As the issue became increasingly more sensitive Roosevelt thought it might kill his bid for presidency. He agreed to support legislation that would enlarge the park by 1.5 million acres, bringing the total land from 4 million to 5.5 million acres. The proposed amendment passed in referendum, expanding the park and eliminating the threat of lumbering. Before the legislation passed, my log cabin was outside of the park; afterward it was 30 miles inside the "blue line." Through this and other issues Apperson had groomed me for the political wars that would follow.

I found during the Moose River fight that many of the existing conservation organizations were unable to act quickly, so I spearheaded a group called the Friends of the Forest Preserve. Headquarters were in my Adirondack Room, and the trustees of this small group were comprised of numerous leaders from the other statewide organizations. We could move immediately and decisively on issues that threatened the wild-forest character of the mountains. Zahniser became our national representative. The group also published *The Forest Preserve*, a small magazine that dealt with the forest preserve. My earlier book, *Defending the Wilderness,* tells about the battles we fought and how we retained the integrity of the "forever wild" covenant in the New York State Constitution.

I can feel the excitement those battles brought to my life as well as the many opportunities that came along with them, such as chairing the Forest Preserve Committee for the New York State Conservation Council and working with the council's extensive system of regional leaders; serving as an advisor for the New York State Legislative Committee on River Regulation for four years, and the New York State Legislative Committee on Natural Resources for fifteen years; and serving as an advisor to numerous state conservation commissioners. I worked with individuals from all walks of life who recognized a higher meaning in the wild-character of the Adirondacks than just exploitation of its natural resources.

During those years, various organizations formed a state-wide coalition—local sportsmen's clubs, women's garden clubs, labor unions, service clubs, churches, and many others. We gave programs using motion picture and slide presentations to literally hundreds of groups across the state. We worked to-gether to create a political voice that the New York State Legis-lature could not ignore. Zahniser added national pressure through the Wilderness Society and other national groups. Gov-ernors and legislative leaders were unusually responsive to the programs the coalition advanced—wilderness tracts where mo-tor vehicles were banned, land-acquisition bond issues, with-drawal of the proposed system of reservoirs, preservation of the Moose River region, the Upper Hudson River, and the establishment of the Wild, Scenic, and Recreational Rivers Sys-tem. In the thirty years the coalition worked together, we did not lose one major legislative battle that threatened the natural resources of this magnificent country.

I remember during the 1950s and 1960s people began to come to the mountains in increasing numbers. Two state ski centers were built (one on Whiteface Mountain and the other on Gore Mountain), the Adirondack Northway was constructed, and the main roads in the park were improved. The Adirondacks became accessible to the millions of people living in cities within a day's drive of the park. Development of back country lands and lake shores seemed inevitable, threatening the wild-forest character of the park. It became apparent that if the park was to be preserved and enhanced, controls on development were needed. In 1969, Governor Nelson Rockefeller created the Tem-porary Commission to Study the Future of the Adirondacks. The commission came up with ideas of monumental signifi-cance, including the creation of a bipartisan, quasi-governmental Adirondack Park Agency that would control development on private lands within the park and cooperate with the New York State Department of Environmental Conservation in the formulation of policies involving state lands. The agency's zoning guidelines were based on the land's ability to withstand use and were the most progressive of any land-use legislation in the United States.

The Adirondack Park Agency has been in existence for more than twenty years and has strived to enhance the wild-forest character of these mountains. It has worked with the Department of Environmental Conservation to add vital tracts to wilderness and wild-forest areas of the forest preserve, and it has introduced conservation easements for private lands. The easements permit public use while providing selective lumber-ing and tax benefits to owners. The work of the agency will remain critical as we move into a new century and undertake to find the balance necessary for man and wilderness to live in harmony. The agency is now responding to the new recommen-dations of Governor Mario M. Cuomo's Commission on the Adirondacks in the Twenty-First Century, which were released in 1991.

The Commission on the Adirondacks in the Twenty-First Century had an advisory committee of nearly 100 respected individuals representing the various constituencies concerned with the Adirondacks and an excellent professional staff. It was challenged to prepare a visonary report of what the Adirondack Park should be like in the twenty-first century. Their report consisted of more than a thousand pages of analy-sis of the park as it exists today and a map outlining what it ideally could be in the future. The report contained many con-troversial suggestions, expected from such a diversified advi-sory committee, but few people anticipated the controversial reception it received. Unfortunately, it was attacked as if it were a plan for immediate implementation rather than one for the future to be thoroughly studied before activated. Time has softened the impact of the report's negative reception as thou-sands of residents in the park sift through it to find the essence of its intent.

The report emphasizes that widespread development within the park would be precluded because of three factors:

1. The natural topography of the park itself—mountains, rivers, lakes, and lowlands—border the several thousands of miles of state road frontage so closely and extensively that only a minimum amount building is possible.

2. The New York State Forest Preserve and other public lands comprise more than one-half of the 9,375 square miles of land within the park. These public lands contain not only the most scenic and accessible lands, and most of them are as unchangeable as a mountain of rock itself.

3. Many large landowners desire scenic or conservation easements from the state; others pride themselves in retaining their clubs and estates that have been in existence for decades. Additional large tracks of land are owned by colleges and lumber companies or are extensive wetlands that are strictly controlled by the state.

While these factors limit development and assure the wild-forest character of the park (which in turn is continually enhanced by the climate and the healing forces of nature), the report strongly recommends establishment of a buffer zone around the periphery of the park. In this buffer zone, on some 2,000 miles of lovely country, where scores of rivers and streams empty into larger rivers and lakes, is where development is being encouraged.

In recent years I have watched new generations of young men and women carry their vision of the Adirondacks to the legislative halls just as I did in my youth. These young people come from all walks of life, from residency inside and outside of the park. They speak out as organized groups or from singular conviction, and they express the strong resurgence of concern about the Adirondack Park. Their voices represent the legions of people who love and care about the region and its global significance. The battles they are waging are as difficult as those we fought. I am proud of their efforts as they continue to preserve the priceless natural heritage of this unique mountain region so that there will always be a frontier for youth to explore.

In Front of the Fire at Beaver House

• • •

The sun is beginning to sink below the spruces on Cataract Mountain. The high peak of Crane is illuminated by its last rays. A cool wind drifts in from the wilderness. Twilight is ending another glorious September day. It is time for the warmth and cheer from the huge stone fireplace in the cabin where the glow of flames of beech and maple enliven the room. A time to spend an evening with friends who love the wilderness as I do. A time for a fine meal. A time to relive adventures of other years or plan for new ones in the months or years to come.

I can go inside now, confident that the youth in the distant tomorrows will backpack down winding forest trails, glimpse the silver of a wilderness lake shining through the trees, and gather around their crackling campfire. They, too, will experience the freedom of spirit and the indescribable happiness found in solitude, enriched by the song of the hermit thrush, the hoot of an owl, or the cry of a loon. They will talk about a climb to a storm-swept mountain summit or a trip down the canyon of a wild river. And before taking to their sleeping bags under starlit heavens, they will talk about how they can make possible similar experiences for the legions of youth who will hunger for adventures as they have. I can go inside knowing that an ancient log cabin, the Beaver House, and Adirondack Cabin Country have played a part in crystallizing this priceless heritage.